A LONDON BOOK WINDOW

A London Book Window
By James Milne

Essay Index Reprint Series

BOOKS FOR LIBRARIES PRESS

FREEPORT, NEW YORK

First Published 1925
Reprinted 1968

LIBRARY OF CONGRESS CATALOG CARD NUMBER:
68-16957

PRINTED IN THE UNITED STATES OF AMERICA

To George Haven Putnam

My dear Putnam:

May I, with that brevity which attests
the soul of sincerity, as well as the soul of
wit, dedicate to you, who, for half a century
and more, have been a great Ambassador of
Letters between the two great English-
speaking peoples, these lights and shadows
of the London Book World, where you
are so well liked; and always, my friend,
I am yours, James Milne:

A SALUTE TO ADVENTURE!

MAY a plea be made for the exploration of the English book-world by anybody who wants a fine adventure? It is still a dark country to many people, may be for no worse reason than that they do not know how to regard it. Other realms are familiar, but this one is the "Erewhon" among them and doesn't happen, or just happens.

Now it is not like that, for nothing just happens, though it is true that surprise is the mother of enterprise. There have always been books, in manuscript or in print, and so they are taken as read—fairy things of nowhere. You may whistle a long time for a fairy and not have it appear, unless you know where to meet it, in the gloaming, its time. You have only to ask for a book and it obliges, gladly and quickly, if you salute it by name, because that manifests friendship, the sweetest word in life, after love.

A SALUTE TO ADVENTURE!

There we fall upon the danger which haunts friendship in all its aspects; that of being taken for granted. Do not commit this foolishness with books, any more than with hearts. Both are spiritual and mental, and together they form the Bourne of the Soul which lies between our world and the other, an eternal romance of two worlds. Yes, when hearts and books are concerned, you must not only be a constant friend but a lover willing to take risks, as all great lovers do, certainly women, for what is womanhood unless the divine emprise, and what would it be if it were not?

There is hope for the explorer in our English book-land the moment he can see it coloured with the rose-blush of a little quite healthy sentiment. No rightly sentimental person would walk up Bond Street in the warmth of noon, or in the coquettish afternoon hour, without wondering, " What's going to happen to me before I get to the other end? " Nothing does happen, as a rule, and, possibly, that is best, but something might happen—you never know!—for Bond Street has a gracious, gallant air, and, with its friendly want of width, so that a glance crosses it, a twice gracious, gallant air; which is all the kindling thought. Well, a like torch of imagination and spirituality is needed for the explor-ation of the English land of books, and in it there will, most surely, be happenings.

It is challenging, as well as charming, for it is full not merely of great names and great deeds, but of surprises of all sorts. The paladin ensign of Shakespeare waves over a field of cloth of gold, on which are blazoned many other names, scarcely less illustrious than his in English authorship. The cloth of gold is spangled with jewels of books, from dignified folios to nimble pocket editions, the trophies of this national authorship. But, if you please, there is something not yet discovered, scarcely, perhaps, suspected—the pasturage behind the panoply.

What is here gravely meant is the warp and woof of England's book-world, its state of being, its throb as a delicate, complicated machine, delivering the goods of literature for whoever will have them. They do not fall from the heavens, so much Provi-dential manna, but have to be cared for, Moses-like, on their pilgrimage, else they might perish. Such is the captivating Canaan which awaits your exploration, offering you colour and incident, fancy

A SALUTE TO ADVENTURE !

*and fact, rhyme and reason, smiles and tears, yea,
a thousand and one satisfactions, as in the Arabian
Nights Entertainments.*

*Will you walk and talk in it with a seasoned
but ever curious traveller who well knows its ways,
the stir of its adventure, the softness of its caress,
the whisper of its confidences, above all the austere
splendour of its beauty, and we shall see what we
shall see, hear what we shall hear ?   Come !*

The Autumn, 1924.   *JAMES MILNE.*

CHAPTERS AND THEIR CONTENTS

CONTENTS

A LONDON BOOK WINDOW

I

WHAT MAKES A "BEST SELLER"

ONE often hears the question, "Why should that particular book be a best seller.? What is there in it?" The answer is, that there is always something human which appeals to a great number of people. "Best sellers" are not made only of dry paper and print. They have a thrill or a tear, a sorrow or a laugh for the multitude. They must, in some form, have the fabled touch of Nature which makes the whole world kin.

What was there in 'If Winter Comes' that captured the general reader, old and young, in our land, in America, wherever the English language is spoken? Surely it was a suffering such as comes to many a man, especially since the war, and the brave seeing of it through. People said of the battered but enduring hero, "That's just like me."

No novel sells in thousands and thousands

unless it has, somewhere in it, a key to the emotions. What passage in human nature drove ' The Sheik ' into a circulation which it would take pages of figures to reckon ? Surely it was its elementary desert love, as between a picturesque man and a dreaming maid, he a brigand of passion, she a captive more and more willing to his compulsion. Young womanhood and young manhood have their visions, and they will seek them in impossible tales, with impossible heroes and heroines, and not be a bit the worse, because to most of us the pleasures of anticipation are the great pleasures, sometimes the only pleasures.

Somebody, it does not matter who, said to a London lady of culture and beauty, who does matter, " Think of you being found reading ' The Sheik,' a perfectly impossible person who never could be on land or sea." " Yes," she answered, laying down the novel beside her tea-cup, " that's just it—the impossible man ! A woman can always meet, may be even get, the possible man. But the impossible man is only possible in an impossible story, and the Eve in a woman's good heart goes out to him."

Human nature, you see, human nature all the time, and the strange thing is that any other general explanation should be sought for " best

4

sellers." When they are great books like, in our
day, Thomas Hardy's ' Tess,' or John Galsworthy's ' Forsyte Saga,' they sail high and never
have the rather slighting name of " best seller."
They are always selling, always being read, and,
being sincere " human documents," they become
documents of life.

But a " best seller," whether of fiction or fact,
a very bold romance, or an unusually frank autobiography, may most likely be the comet of a
season. It has a tang which takes people, an
anecdotage which retails at a dinner party, or it
is launched at a psychological moment in public
opinion and, hey presto, as jugglers cry, the
trick is done.

" Where are the leaves of yester-year ? " Yes,
and where are the " best sellers," many of them,
anyhow, of yester-year ? Dead and behanged,
like the red-handed pirates sung about in ' Treasure Island.' Oh, well, it is the way of all nature,
literary nature included, to bud, to bloom and
to die. But if the roots of true-written treasure
be present, there will come a second blooming,
and with a little luck, it may be everlasting.

One thinks of two " best seller " books, an
English novel and a Scottish memoir, which were
safe, the hour they were born, to become ever-

lasting, because they are idylls of motherhood. The novel is Mrs. Henry Wood's ' East Lynne,' over which mothers still cry, for the reason that it touches every string of their hearts. The memoir is Sir James Barrie's ' Margaret Ogilvy,' a portrait which will probably survive when all the characters of his plays, unless it be Peter Pan, lose themselves in the mists of time. Why ? It is a portrait not alone of Barrie's mother, but of the Scottish mother, and, with differences caused by environment, she is the universal mother, the supreme heroine of all our affections, an unfailing conduct to a " best seller " in the worthy sense.

II

THE HAPPY ENDING

WE have all, at one time or another, sung "There is a happy land, far, far away," and it has done us good. We have all believed, also, in the "happy ending" to a story, and that faith has done us no harm. The "happy ending" has, indeed, been much to the English novel, and now it is to be discarded, even derided, by a growing number of writers. That is hard news, my friends, and why should there be occasion for it?

Well, the very clever young novelist, and the very clever young reader, are both, in a measure, responsible for this thing. You generally find that it needs two of anything to make trouble, except, perhaps, when there are three, and then it is worse trouble. Whatever happens in a human way is pretty sure to have its counterpart in a literary way, because the last is an echo of the first, or should be if it is worth its salt.

7

Anyhow, the young novelist, a ruthless fellow, or a daring maiden, as the case may be, is nowadays at daggers-drawn with the " happy ending," unless, of course, the dream is " Oh, to be popular, popular, popular ! " and then it must be permitted. Is it that our young novelists are less sentimental than the novelists of other days ? Is it that they have a deeper grip of life as it really is, or is it merely that they think themselves cleverer than those who have gone before them ?

Probably the note which would make away with the " happy ending " derives from all those elements and from others. Mostly, may be, it comes from the terrible plague of cleverness which glisters in every second story that one happens upon. It used to be character, the heart, the soul, the something greater than brains, that made a story which was a story. They remain the big things, and they will always be the big things, but it was new to drive hard cleverness across them, and newness has its inviting cry, though, on occasion, the harvest can be ever so empty.

Now, all that suggests, however faintly, the drum of the young writer beating against the ark of the covenant, as once it was thought to be, called the " happy ending." Why should youth at the pen not take its own road to be youth at the helm ? Why not, especially when, beyond the wall there are ever so many young readers waiting for a message which they cannot themselves put into words, the message that realism lives as well as romance. True, but what we have come to, with some of our young writers, is that the unhappy ending is thought more faithful to life and to art than the " happy ending."

Think round the circle of your own friends and see if they are in as bad a state as that. There is Pleasant, who is engaged to a decent lad, and they will be married when he has got on his feet and she has added a few more summers to her twenty. There is Harry, middle-aged, the husband of a contented wife, the father of a boy and girl, and all is well and fair in that household. There is Rosalind, a grandmother, who holds to the poetry of her Christian name, but, as the years go down hill, becomes more and more glad that she tacked plain Smith on to it, because he is her " John Anderson, my Joe."

Doesn't that rather rosy picture stand for your friends as you know them ? It stands better, anyhow, than a picture of strife and desertion and divorce would do, and it is sweeter to have for company. The world is neither all bright nor all drab, but a mixture of both, with cross-currents constantly flowing. This means that a story ending may be happy, or unhappy, or a tangled thread of the two. But don't let us be told that the unhappy ending is righter than the other, and, very particularly, don't let us have it forced upon the reader as a trade-mark of quality in fiction. There is a tendency to do that among small groups of writers who live spiritually by the incense which is common to them all.

It is good, no doubt, to be clever and defying, but it is not good to be grating and intolerant. Nay, it is not good business, any more than it is good literature, because judgment is in the hands of the public who really, at the end of the day, make literary reputations. This public takes no notice of embellishments. It goes straight to the depths, and asks :

" Has the man anything to say to me ? Has he a message ? Is he sincere ? Does he know ?

If the answer is ' Yes ' on those and like counts, then bring him in with his novel and set him and it in the best easy-chair, and we shall listen gladly. But if he is merely Mr. Clever Clever, and determined to show it by having an unhappy ending, then we don't want him."

THE HAPPY ENDING

It is a tangled affair this of the " happy ending," but if you would like to know a secret,
for, of course, you can keep it, listen ! The
" happy ending " is not really going to be outed,
not by a long way, and you say, " Thank good-
ness for that " ; and so say all of us. Even our
terrifying young novelists secretly love it, and
when they get a little older, more mellow and
sunshiny, they will patronize it, for that's the
way of the world.

III

THE DECAY OF HEROES

IT is time that something frank and honest were said about the hero and heroine of the present-day novel. They are not what they were, and one can say that without recalling the immortal deliverance about 'Punch' : " He's not what he was ! " and the answer, " No, he never was ! " Truly, the state of the English hero of English fiction is far from good, and the lady in the case is equally doubtful.

Do you ever, nowadays, hear anybody speak of a story hero as if he were an actual person ? People used to do that, you know. Heroes were real half a century ago when the great Victorian writers were in command. Charles Dickens and William Makepeace Thackeray were the parents of imaginary children who, like the soul of John Brown of Ossawatomie, still go marching on. Has anybody, within easy memory, created a large, red-blooded, all-appealing hero who goes marching on, or off, or does anything else that much matters ?

No answer ! There is none, because the average novel of to-day practically has no hero, unless, indeed, the person who writes it. We know, or, at all events, a proverb tells us, that no man is a hero to his own valet. That leaves lots of openings for heroes, because so few people have valets. Anyhow, this hole in human nature, always a frail and tender plant, is filled by the fact that every author may be a hero to his own novel.

The clumsiest way of setting about this is to take your own unprofitable story, or as much of it as will stand print and a " jacket " in colours, and bravely write it. Bravery is needed because, often enough, there is nothing else. You must, of course, invent a little, if, unlike George Washington, you can tell a lie. You must also embellish a good deal ; but that is easy, because we are all embellishers now, certainly, when we are not embalmers of the literary corpses of others.

You will begin to see how it is that, with a process of this sort going on, the fine old hero of other days has been reduced to cinema and ashes. A true hero never could have many brains, only brawn and beauty, and even they

13

are not left to him. The poor fellow has become a neurotic, a spiritualist, a lady-killer, anything you like, for his heroic qualities have fallen from him like withered laurels. He is no more a hero of the helmet and the toga, of the bold heart and the high mind, of the slogan, borrowed from Sir Walter Scott, who made it for real heroes, " Come one, come all, this rock shall fly from its firm base as soon as I."

The modern hero is early in flight ; but then he is no hero at all, only what on the stage they call a " leading man," and our heroines, bless you, are in a very corresponding mess, though it makes one seem unchivalrous to say so. Here we come plump against the woman novelist, because she should have looked after the traditional heroine, and she hasn't. Not merely that ; she mocks at her, jeers at her, calls her, when she takes any notice of her at all, old-fashioned and stupid. Well, may be it is a true bill.

But wasn't there something appealing in the young woman who never did anyone any harm, not even herself ; in the middle-aged woman who was just content to be a wife and mother ; in the woman of grave years who not only didn't mind being a grandmother, but was proud of it ? They are all dead and buried, so far as the completely up-to-date twentieth century novelist is concerned, for he only deals with the problems and troubles that sent them to their graves where, at least, they have peace.

A queer kind of young writer is about who thinks he can give a new form and a new expression to English literature, including the novel, for he makes no reserves. He puts his money on himself, and when the bet is honoured by a guileless public, as it often is, he thinks the world well won. Perhaps, but that is the road of destruction for heroines, who, if they are to be worthy of the word, need the prayers of sincerity, not the light-o'-love of mockery. Nowadays a heroine is, in ordinary course, made a bit of a baggage, labelled " handle with care," left to shift for herself, and so does she fall and fall, both in true human nature and in true artistry, that nobody knows what her last state may be, except that it is bound to be much worse than her first, her original state.

Where rests the secret of all this wrongness about the hero and the heroine of to-day's generally accepted novel ? Why, in two things, which are that never were such a set of smart amateurs writing the English novel and that, as a consequence, it is mostly a novel without plan or plot or characterization. The amateur novelist has got to be abated wherever found, and he certainly turns up in strange places. Until he is abated, we shall be tortured with small originalities of style and manner ; and heroes and heroines will merely be the puppets of their authors' good conceit of themselves. Unfortunately an English woman, as well as an English man, sometimes lacks the saving grace of humour which is natural to the " unspeakable Scot ! "

IV

COLOUR AND READING

W E know that in Nature there is a colouration which hides wild things against
other wild things and against man. The par-
tridge is brown, and so might be a small dot on
the brown fields where it is to be found. The
brown hare of the Scottish uplands becomes
bluish-white in the winter, and even the eye of
an eagle in flight might miss it among the snow.

Nature has wise ways which are taken for
granted, but you would hardly fancy that colouration comes into our reading. A well-known
novelist once said, speaking of his own ways of
writing, " I think in pictures." That is colouration in the creation of literature, and if we are to
have anything but so much pedestrian writing, it
has to be present, for it means passion, action,
everything that makes a book human and readable.

Again, however, that is not what here really

concerns us, because this is the call of certain colours of binding, more than others, to readers. A scholarly man likes a green binding, because it is quiet, and helps him to be what he is after being, reflective. A poet or an artist likes a soft neutral binding, perhaps because it has no element in it to disturb self-communion. A traveller or a hunter likes a cover of a substantial colour, but he will lighten it with, say, a picture of hunting trophies done in gold. You will find on the cover of the Marquess Curzon's ' Tales of Travel ' a reproduction of a very brilliant Order which Abdur, once the Ameer of Afghanistan, designed and gave to him.

It is, however, when we come to novels and to women, the great readers of them, that we reach colouration in book-bindings at its psychological height. You will know the London libraries of Mudie and Smith, of the ' Times ' Book Club, and Boots, for they are all great institutions in the circulation of books. Suppose you visit one of them, keep an eye on the shelves from which novels may be chosen by readers, and see how the choice runs.

Almost to a certainty, a woman will first put her hand on a novel which has a red binding. If you were to ask her why, she could not tell you, for she makes her choice instinctively. Is it that red betokens the kind of novel which she wants, something with the adventure of womanhood in it ? Possibly. Anyhow, she will open the novel, look rapidly at a page or two, and either decide to take it or not to take it. It is extraordinary how rapidly one can get the atmosphere of a novel, and if it be all right, the characters may take care of themselves, and they will do so.

One thinks of the harmless jingle, " The rose is red, the violet's blue, sugar's sweet, and so are you," because it takes us to the next colour most popular with a woman in search of a novel. It is blue and, for some reason, a light blue, such as you may see about when the streets are gay with summer frocks and the sun shines. Blue, of course, is " love true," or, at all events, there is a tradition that it stands for that and ever so much " sweetness and light."

Perhaps we have in this tradition and association the explanation why a blue book-cover comes next to a red one in drawing power. It expresses romance while it is young and care-free, before it has been gnarled with the " problems " which find their expression in red. Quite likely, then, it is the young woman, rather than the other woman, who most patronizes the blue binding.

She sees in it her dreams and visions, as they swim poetically before her young eyes, and she hopes, when she opens the book, to find herself " within the blue."

But, if she be a girl still on the brink of womanhood, you will discover that, though the blue cover has taken her psychologically, she will apply another test to the story before she decides to read it. She glances, for a moment, at the opening pages, and they do not carry the elements of decision for her, that they carry to the older woman. She wants to have some idea what she is going to read, because there is no sense in taking home a book that won't be interesting. Even so she will gamble a little on that if she is sure the end will be " fair and well," meaning that it will be a happy ending. She does not wish to spoil her reading by knowing just how things work out in detail, but she likes to feel that they do work out in marriage bells, or in re-unions, not in tragedies such as some of our young " realists " insist upon having.

It is red, then, for full-blown romance, in, shall we say, the Byronic spirit ? It is blue for the love of girls, and the heroes, handsome, manly, gentlemen every inch of them, who are in their hearts. The third colour of asking is green, and how are we to work out the strata of psychology which gives it that place ?

Is it that readers who neither see red nor blue concentrate on green as being a colour into which they may read anything, or read nothing ? " Green grow the rushes, o' ; long live the lasses, o'," sang Robert Burns, but nothing can be more demure than greenery. Possibly, then, many people choose " green mansions " in a bookish way, because they are most comfortable, alike to the mind and the eye. It is a happiness of book-land that you can find every colour in it, as well as every sort of adventure for the mind, the heart and the soul.

Somebody will ask, does the three-colour test as to novels and ladies hold when a bookshop and the buying of books are concerned, not just a circulating library and borrowing ? Yes and No. Yes, in the sense that if the psychology of the business came into play the outcome would be the same. But, No, for the reason that novels laid out in a bookshop are all in their " jackets," and, therefore, one does not see the colour of bindings unless these are removed.

A consequence of this " blanketing," as one may term it, is that " jackets " are now playing their part in influencing the choice of readers.

Originally they were plain and intended to do no more than protect the book within, from the rigour and dirt of our London climate. Now they have become " things of beauty," and some of them might even be a joy for ever, so charming are they. Many clever artists give us many clever designs, and always the thing is to have a calling picture, the hero, the heroine, or a striking incident from the story.

" Jackets " could not be the success they are without cutting into the colour privileges of the bindings, but they will never usurp those privileges. One's acquaintance with a " wrapper " may be an affair of a few moments, but with a binding it covers time, because it implies the reading of the book. Therefore the literary tricolour of red, blue and green is likely to go on waving from the top shelves and other shelves of libraries, no matter how attractively, and many-coloured, " jackets " may be turned out. It is a tricolour which, lightly though it has been presented, has a real psychological basis in human nature, and that is the ultimate reason why it will go on waving.

V

THE "PROBLEM" NOVEL

NOWADAYS we never hear anybody say "Problem Novel." It simply isn't done. And what has brought us to this is rather interesting, as we shall see.

Some folk will tell you, "No, we don't speak about it because the name isn't nice, any more than the novel." Others, with a literary turn, will say, "Oh, it is dead, the problem novel. So why speak about it?" A third company may observe, "Ah, a labelled 'problem novel' couldn't be very agreeable, but it's gone, so let us accept a well-known Latin tag and of the dead speak nothing but good." None of those histories in brief, takes us along the right road of explanation, or, at all events, far enough along it.

One has to go back a long way to see that road wind, like the river of Swinburne's poem, "Somewhere safe to sea," back even to the 'Nineties, when we were all young and being

23

deliciously " shocked." It was an experience
which would have had no bashfulness for the
young fellows and young girls of this prancing
hour, and therefore they miss something.

They miss the small earthquake which rent
London Town when Sarah Grand set her ' Heavenly Twins ' flying. They miss the other earthquake of Mrs. Mannington Caffyn's ' Yellow
Aster,' and they miss Grant Allen's famous " Hill-
top " novel, which scaled a literary Mount Pis-
gah of the period and saw the promised land of
woman's emancipation lying beyond.

What happened was that a slow-gathering
wave of candour towards the eternal problems
of human nature, broke on the worn rocks of
Victorianism. Similarly, there rose, like a chorus,
what had been the still, small voices of the women
crying in the wilderness for political rights comparable to those possessed by men.

It is only fair to the " problem novel " years
to say that they meant this mixture of the humanities and the justices, and that the two influences
marched forward together. If they had not, if
they had marched separately, or at different times,
they might have fallen by the way and that, as
we can now perceive, through the glass of fuller
knowledge, would not have been good.

THE " PROBLEM " NOVEL

It was a difficult job to create a meeting-place between the old-fashioned novel, which dealt only in convention, and the new "problem novel," which insisted on being "life." Often this was no novel at all, in the sense of a plot, characters, and artistry, but just a tract. Sometimes it was sloppy and neurotic, and, to use no harder word, unsweet.

No matter, it persisted, shocking the dying Victorians, though they read it—or how did they know what it was like?—enticing the non-Victorians because it spelt " spiciness," as well as progress. Why, a gifted lady of title who was young then, as she is still beautiful, called every Saturday morning at a well-known West-End book-shop and, always in the same words, said, " Give me a ' spicy ' novel for the week-end."

Now, if that was the kind of atmosphere which the " problem novel " created in its heyday, if it was a literary red rag, in two ways, to multitudes of people, what has become of it ? If, in its early convulsions, it helped to pull down the temple of the old three-volume novel, surely it cannot just have withered silently away. If it made sermons and parables, exhortations and denouncements, it must have planted its footprints in the sands of time. It did all those things, with the consequent results, and yet we have forgotten to speak its name, much less to whisper fearfully that name in a drawing-room.

What has happened ? It is all quite simple, all perfectly natural, as most things appear, when we survey them backwards. The " problem novel " of thirty years ago was often raw, and it said things and implied things which hurt. Minds were sensitive, or thought themselves sensitive to the newer, higher, better, braver school of human knowledge which was coming along. So there was a clash, almost a ferment, in opinion, but, with the passing years, relative values found their due places, and now those values are stabilized.

By this it is meant that the quality of novel writing is much finer than it was, speaking of the average story. It is a poor writer now who could not handle the most delicate problems of the heart, the soul, the mind, or the body, and yet be reticently artistic. Our writers and our readers have learned to think aloud, and dis-covered that Nature, in all her ways, is beauty, if she is rightly interpreted. It is prying, half-clothed mystery, that makes trouble, and with that the current reader is impatient, even angry, so that coarseness in a book makes dead against its sale.

The English novel has risen away from the rude " problem novel," and the young English generation has bound white wings to its knowledge in everything. Those two movements have, in their coming together, simply crushed out the " problem novel" as a material thing. Spiritually, and as literature, it is universally with us, only we never name it, and it would be misleading and unnecessary to do so. To-day, it is just a novel, that and no more or less, and so a literary mystery is cleared up.

VI

CONSIDERED LITERARY TRIFLES

DO you like to hear about the little things which go on in the book world ? It is a commonplace that the small things of life are often the vital things. They can be, in the book world, as elsewhere, and therefore they are not only interesting, they are important.

When John, Viscount Morley—as he liked to be called, keeping his familiar Christian name—made his will, he ordered that there should be no biography of him. He also ordered that nobody should have access to his papers ; and some people said, " But is that right, because those papers must concern other public men and public affairs ? "

Now John Morley is not the first great man who has said, " I want no biography." Thackeray said it, with the result that we have no life of him, only scraps. George Meredith said it. And even Mr. Asquith, who has a quiet, tolerant philosophy, tells us that he will do his best to stand in the way of a biography of himself.

Obviously a man may refuse to have a biography, but he cannot prevent anybody writing about him from the available sources of information. John Morley's view was that he had sufficiently told his life-story in his 'Recollections,' that his books were always the evidence of him as a literary man, and, finally, that any State papers with which he was associated would, in due time, be accessible in the National Departments to which they belong.

There, in a personal instance, we have the two sides of a question often likely to arise in English literature. A new series of Queen Victoria's letters is being selected by Mr. George Earle Buckle, whom we knew for long as editor of 'The Times.' It will be in his discretion to say what can wisely be published and what should not be published, and where there is any doubt he will probably take the opinion of the King.

The late Mr. Baring-Gould, who was the author of many novels and other books, wrote his memories. Doing so, he found for them a very apt motto in Plato : "What we learn in childhood takes a wonderful hold on the memory. With respect to myself, I am not certain that I could recall the whole of yesterday's discourse, but I should be very much astonished if anything I had heard a long time ago, were to escape my remembrance."

Think what England and the world were like when, as a boy of thirteen, he went with his parents to St. Malo, in France, across the Narrow Seas from the Channel Islands. "We took our carriage," he says, "but not our horses with us from Plymouth." A year earlier he had been at school at Warwick, and, being delicate, he was taken to his dancing-classes in a sedan-chair. There, indeed, we have a glimpse of the past, and perhaps distance lends enchantment to it.

Some forty years ago Gladstone was visiting somewhere in England, and he was shown a book called ' Country Conversations,' which had been printed for private circulation only. Quite recently it was made public through Mr. John Murray, but still without any name on the title-page. There is always a natural curiosity to know the authorship of an anonymous book which is really interesting, so who wrote this one ?

We heard, when the book was being discussed, that it was by a relative of Mr. Bridgeman, the Home Secretary in Mr. Baldwin's Government. The arrangements for its being given public print were, in fact, made by him, and there he did a service to those who like to read about the humours and the realities of English country life at its best.

Still, we were without the name of the writer ; but so knit together, though so spacious, is the book world that you will find her named in Mrs. Asquith's "Autobiography." When she was a girl she was a great friend of the Gladstone family, and during a conversation with the " G.O.M." he spoke of being shown ' Country Conversations.' He said that it was very good, and that it was by a Miss Tollet, no doubt, a quiet English lady living in the country and desiring no celebrity.

Miss Tollet may or may not care for the recognition her book has received from a younger generation which likes to read about Victorian England, though it does not always admit as much. One hopes that she may not have other people claiming that they wrote ' Country Conversations,' for, strange as it may seem, such things have happened.

When Mr. Coulson Kernahan brought out his ' Dead Man's Diary,' a book far too human and spiritual ever to die, he did so anonymously. He meant that it should remain anonymous, but so many people claimed to be its author that he had to declare himself. A rather subtle way in which one man made the claim was to take a manuscript to a publisher and say, " You see I wrote ' A Dead Man's Diary.' "

When, in 1906, Miss Marjorie Bowen had a hit with her ' Viper of Milan,' there was the immediate request, " Who is she ? " but nobody else claimed to be " Marjorie Bowen." It was a writing name, for the real name of the authoress, then hardly more than a girl, was Miss Gabrielle Margaret Vere Campbell. Her father was the son of a gifted Harley Street doctor, and her mother, Mrs. Vere Campbell, was a writer of good novels, a gift which passed on to " Marjorie Bowen."

She is now Mrs. Arthur Long, and she and her husband and their three children have a beautiful old house in Kent. There " Marjorie Bowen " writes her stories, and there she finds inspiration for them, especially as lately she has turned more to modern fiction. Her series of historical romances have occupied her most of her life, and they are a testimony to the quality and the vitality that still belong to that great branch of English literature on which Sir Walter Scott set his seal.

Another historical novelist to whom we owe much, some of us think ever so much, is Mr. Stanley Weyman, who has recently achieved a remarkable feat. A quarter of a century ago, or more, he rapidly made a name with his ' Gentleman of France,' his ' Under the Red Robe,' and the other stories which we link with them. When he had written so many—as many, he thought, as he cared to write—he folded up his literary tent, went to live in the Principality of Wales, and said, " I'll write no more."

But if a man has a rich vein of authorship in him, that is not the end, and it was not to be the end with Mr. Stanley Weyman. When he had rested for years, material for novels gathered again in his mind. Next there came, as there naturally comes, the desire to shape that material into something. Thus it is that we have had a new series of stories from Mr. Stanley Weyman and may he go on. His triumph is that he has won back to the place his first series got him, and that is not an easy thing to do.

There is, as a matter of truth, a large element of chance, good luck, ill luck, or whatever you like to call it, about the book calling, whether it be that of an author or that of a publisher. No book of the past few years has been better read than Mr. Ernest Bramah's ' Wallet of Kai Lung,' and no book has more deserved it. Well, ever so many publishers had it through hand and refused it before it came to the desk of Mr. Grant Richards. When he did publish the book, it went very slowly at first, and it was only after it had received sincere praise from a dozen well-known men of letters that it took the public.

Perhaps the late Mr. W. H. Hudson's best book is his ' Green Mansions,' and one remembers how heartily Sir William Robertson Nicoll bore testimony to its qualities. Would you believe that Hudson had hawked the manuscript round the publishers until he was tired of it and they were tired both of it and him ? It is something of a rule in literature that recognition comes most slowly to the very best work.

This is not only natural, but inevitable, because the higher you go in writing, the fewer are there with the insight to recognize it. If genius be in the case, then that is still more difficult, because it means originality, and the average person, even the quite intelligent person, has no use for originality, until it has fought its way through to acceptance.

There were originality and power, if not beauty, in a Scottish novel, entitled ' The House with the

Green Shutters,' which cut, with a raw bump, into the prosperous years of the " kailyard " story. Behind the name, " George Douglas " on the book, there was another name, that of Brown. The author, therefore, was George Douglas Brown, a very clever Scotsman, who died comparatively young. Present-time readers may care to know that, because the novel has been re-issued for their benefit. They will find it a study of the " dour " side of the Scottish character, and they will lament, perhaps, that George Douglas Brown did not live to give us, with the undoubted literary power which was his, a story picture of the more radiant, more prevalent side of Scottish character.

It is easy to follow George Douglas Brown's selection of a pen-name, because he had only to drop the last word of his actual name and there it was. Why other writers have chosen other names is, however, more difficult to understand ; and especially there is the curious case of the American writer " O. Henry," whose short stories have been having a great vogue in England.

His real name was Sidney Porter, he was a bank-teller in an American bank, and, quite undeservedly, he got into trouble. When he began to write, he naturally sought for a *nom de guerre*, and there has been endless guessing as to how he hit on " O. Henry."

A likely enough explanation comes from America, and it takes " O. Henry " to Central America on some visit. There he met a port superintendent whose name was Henery, and to whom friends, when they wanted him, would say, " O, Henery." Being asked about the matter, he said he had lighted upon a volume, ' Cabbages and Kings,' which could only have been written by himself or Sid Porter, because no one else knew the inside history which it contained.

" We used," the port superintendent has also said, " to bunk together near the edge of the bush. Those were lively days, and it was bad manners to come within gunshot range without giving your name and business. So the boys used to ride through the jungle, stop at the edge, and call " O, Mr. Henery ! " or " O, Henery ! "

A small but interesting matter like that suggests the intimate association there now is between authorship in England and in America. It is not only " hands across the sea," but pens across the sea, in the fullest sense of the word. Not merely does the red streak of a kindred blood unite the English people and the American

36

people. The black streak of ink, written as manuscript and then printed in books, is also a great and ever-growing link.

When Mr. H. G. Wells did his 'Outline of History,' nobody but himself had much belief in it. "Why this," it was asked, "when there are already so many history books to which people can turn?" "Ah, but there's nothing like this," Mr. Wells might have said, "nothing complete and popular, nothing just right for the reader of to-day." Therefore he went on, and the 'Outline of History' was not only a triumph, but it begat a growing literature of "Outlines," and so put a footnote to the Romance of Books.

Now, Mr. Wells' 'Outline of History' was a high success here, but it was a great triumph in America, though there many good bookmen were rather wary about its possibilities, perhaps because it was a new idea. There is risk in having a new literary idea even in a progressive country like America, for it observes many mental conventions, as it observes other conventions in its Constitution.

VII

THE ROMANCE OF BOOKS

YOU like books, to read them, to hear about them, to talk about them, perhaps, for who knows all things, even to write them ? Has it occurred to you that every book has one history before it is written, another history after it is written, and possibly a romance or a tragedy thrown in. What I mean is that with books there always goes a little gamble of surprise. We like, in life, the thought, " You never know what may happen." It is equally present in the book-world and equally likeable.

Suppose, though, that I illustrate all this by a perfectly true story about Blackmore's fine and familiar story, ' Lorna Doone.' You might think that, with its colour, its action, and its calling people, it was safe from all mischances and sure of all the good chances. That was not so, and therefore it is an outstanding token of luck, or the want of luck, in our English bookland.

38

THE ROMANCE OF BOOKS

' Lorna Doone ' was published away back in the years when the three-volume novel, ' The Three Decker,' as Rudyard Kipling calls it in a poem, was the " only certain packet for the Islands of the Blest " :

> " Full thirty foot she towered, from waterline to rail,
> It cost a watch to steer her, and a week to shorten sail ;
> But, spite all modern notions, I found her first and
> best—
> The only certain packet for the Islands of the Blest."

' Lorna Doone ' was sent into the world by Mr. Sampson Low, and what then happened to it I heard from his young partner and my old friend, the late Mr. Edward Marston. It made no great hit as a " three volumer," for one reason because Blackmore was only on the edge of his success and so not very well known. But Mr. Sampson Low, a man with the fine balance of literary and business talent which makes a good publisher, was sure of the quality of the romance, sure also that it would win fame if he could once get it going.

What should he do ? He decided on a course which was unusual in his day, namely, to immediately give ' Lorna Doone ' a second birth, as you might say, in a single volume form. He put the disappointment of the " three volumer " in his pocket, set the tale of the Doones afloat as a small craft, and waited to see what would happen.

What did happen was something that neither he nor anybody else could have imagined. The engagement of Queen Victoria's daughter, Princess Louise, to the then Marquis of Lorne, the late Duke of Argyll, happened to be announced in the newspapers. The splendid British public somehow associated the royal romance with ' Lorna Doone,' or ' Lorna Doone' with the royal romance, it matters not which, and bought the novel like hot cakes.

Yes, that, quite plainly told, was the good fortune which befell Blackmore's masterpiece, as we think it, though he himself preferred his other story, ' Springhaven,' a romance of Surrey. One would scarcely say that it would not have come into its own but for the accidental glow of a royal wedding. One may say, however, that it would not have done so as quickly and as fully ; and it might even, sad to think, have missed its ship, as lots of good books have done, and gone down into the literary ocean of oblivion, unheralded and unsung.

To speak of ' Lorna Doone' has been to send one back on the years, not an invitation which eager youth always likes. But it was worth while, wasn't it? And anyhow, I am going to atone by telling you the, in another way, not less romantic history of a book of our day, Florence Barclay's ' Rosary,' which, as you know, has been a tremendous " best seller," both in England and in America.

Mrs. Barclay wrote it during the months she was compelled to lie on her back after a strain from over-taxing her strength at cycling. She wrote it in the quiet rectory where she and her husband then lived in Hertfordshire. She had always a turn for setting things down, and also, what is far rarer, the natural gift of story-telling. It pleased her to write this tale, as it helped to pass the time, and going on a visit to her sister, Mrs. Ballington Booth, in America, she took the manuscript with her.

" Oh," she said one morning, " I have a sort of a novel which I've done, and I wish you'd look at it. You see," she added in such words to her sister, " you are an experienced author and can advise me, and perhaps show what I have done to your own publisher, Mr. Putnam."

So things fell out, for Mrs. Ballington Booth liked ' The Rosary,' and Mr. George Haven Putnam and his advisers liked it, and it went to the printers, then to the binders, and finally came forth a book. When it did, America at once took to the song of ' The Rosary,' and it rang over the American continent as swiftly as a more recent, less beautiful song about bananas and other vegetables. With the vogue of the song there flew the fame of the story, the two so intermixed that it was difficult to say which was which.

Meanwhile a like pageant of success had begun in England, where ' The Rosary ' had been simultaneously published by the Putnams. The English vogue and the American vogue were distinct and different, and yet one held out a hand of assistance, as it were, to the other, because, although the Atlantic is wide, a popular work will always bridge it. Quickly ' The Rosary ' became the " best seller " of two worlds, and if, as we have seen, it had its luck, it also had the qualities to make that luck good, always a necessary condition of prosperity.

The publishers of ' Lorna Doone ' and of ' The Rosary ' had good fortune, as they deserved it, but sometimes that fickle jade goes by when she might well be captured. A little story, which has been whispered among literary gossips, about Mrs. Elinor Glyn's ' Visits of Elizabeth ' and the late William Heinemann, illustrates this kind of happening.

THE ROMANCE OF BOOKS

Mrs. Glyn was new to authorship when she brought her ' Visits of Elizabeth ' to the Heinemann house, where it got courteous attention. Mr. Heinemann was a born publisher, and especially he had that indefinable quality, *flair*, which also makes a journalist. He managed, somehow, to know about all the likely manuscripts that came to his number of Bedford Street, near by the Strand, and he liked ' The Visits of Elizabeth.'

So, without delay, he said he would publish it if Mrs. Glyn would make certain changes which he and his men of letters thought would improve the story. She, however, did not think well of the changes, and took her story to Mr. Gerald Duckworth, in Henrietta Street. He accepted it straight away, it brought her name and fame, and he has published for her ever since.

A quite recent drama of literature has been the burning of a diary left by William Heinemann, which would have made a distinctive and interesting book and which now goes on to the Never Never Shelf of the English book world. Those of us who knew Mr. Heinemann know what a vital personality he was, how wide his contact with authors was, and therefore what intimate conversations and personal vignettes that diary must have contained. No doubt it was the diffi-

43

culty of printing such confidences that led his relatives, into whose care the journal finally came, to have it burned, like Byron's.

When he died, Mr. Heinemann left it to his old friend and partner, Mr. Sidney Pawling, who was shortly to follow him across the unknown border. Once or twice the latter spoke about it, each time wondering what he was to do with it. He indicated that there were parts of the journal which might very well be given to the public, and, on the ground of interest, should be given. But there were other parts too confidential for publicity, and the problem was to select and edit, a problem which Mr. Heinemann had not faced in his own lifetime.

The consequence was that Mr. Pawling did nothing, which, may be, was what most of us would have done in the circumstances. Here was good reading about Wagner and Whistler, Maeterlinck and Max Nordau, Bernard Shaw and Max Beerbohm, and many other literary and artistic celebrities. But what to give and what not to give, that was the rub ! Now a blazing fire has settled it all, some admirable first-hand memoirs have gone up in smoke, and there is no more to be said.

There is another kind of book that never materializes, the book which a writer would, in his heart, like to write, but which, in his mind, he knows he never will write. Our friend Sir William Robertson Nicoll had, all his life, been gathering material for a new, up-to-date history of British journalism. He had done the same for a biographical work on eminent Scotsmen, because, to the end, though he had long dwelt in England, he remained a true, pure Scot, devoted to his native country. He was conscious, perhaps, that he could never in his busy life achieve those two monumental books. But he liked to think of them, to work for them, and possibly the materials he collected may be sifted to us by another hand.

John Morley was, at one time in his life, deeply taken by the rise of the New Italy under Garibaldi, Mazzini and Cavour. He made up his mind to write a history of the uniting of a scattered Italy into a great nation, and he waited hopefully for the opportunity to come. It never came, but it gladdened him to see a son of his old friend and colleague, Sir George Trevelyan, another veteran of English letters and politics, become our modern historian of the New Italy.

A popular figure of the worlds of journalism, literature, and politics, Mr. T. P. O'Connor, made his first hit by deliberately sitting down and writing a life of Benjamin Disraeli. It was a hard task, a big task, because materials were not easy to get, and " Dizzy," who was then alive, was not likely to fling them at an unknown young Irishman. But " T. P." was interested in the character and personality of the Jewish leader of English Conservatism. He gave endless pains and much time to the elucidation of him, and the result was a book which was widely read, and which made " T. P.'s " writing gifts known. Why, by the way, should we not have a new edition of this biography, for it might well be read beside the fuller official one of Disraeli.

We do have available Dean Farrar's ' Life of Christ,' and we think it based on a quite conservative reading of Scripture. You may, however, care to know that when Dr. Farrar wrote it, to the order of a well-known publishing house, it was thought over-advanced. He took it to another house, to Cassells, of La Belle Sauvage Yard, and they have been sending it forth in print ever since. Its success was not less than the success which the Italian, Giovanni Papini's, very different study of Christ was to have in our immediate day, and indeed, to many people, Dean Farrar's name will come back most clearly as the author of his striking study of Christ.

THE ROMANCE OF BOOKS

One might go on talking about the surprises, the chances, the romances, the tragedies, which attend the writing and the publishing of books. It is a fascinating subject, because it proves that the business of the pen is not dull at any point. Always the penman and the publisher will be asking, like the child, "And what happens next ?" Something always does happen. What it is to be you must wait and see ; but it will be worth while waiting.

VIII

FIRST NOVELS AND NOVELISTS

FIRST novels and " first novelists " have always interested me, and why not ? No things in the world have the interest, the beauty, the thrills of first things, whether they be a baby or a book. May be that is why it is so splendid to succeed with a first effort at fiction. None of the successes which come afterwards, good though they may be, can ever compare with the first fine fragrance.

There are two ways in which a first novel may succeed, two ways at least, and when one says that, one is speaking of talented writers, not of genius, for when it comes along it cuts its own swathe, fearing not and caring little whether it earns benediction or anathema.

A novel may be a work of art and so lift the writer's name high, making it only a question of time when he, or she, shall also become successful in the sense of circulation. This was how

48

the beginning of fame, and therefore the beginning of prosperity, although it was long on the road, came to Joseph Conrad with his ' Almayer's Folly.'

The other way is to write a first novel which shall take the public by the heart, even if the critics do not have anything very great to say about it. Of course the perfect way to become a " first novelist " is to blend the two sets of qualities and be at once a " best seller " and a classic ; only that is unusual.

What are the troubles which braid the way ? They are plentiful. For myself, I would, almost certainly, set out without knowing just where my plot was going. That would land me, about the middle of the story, in flops and wobbles and all manner of emergencies. Perhaps about there the reader would get tired of me, and so I would not be a successful " first novelist."

Possibly, being a little hazy about my plot, I should also be a little hazy about my characters, with the result that they would be a company— I hope a pleasant and interesting company— instead of a family of highly distinctive individuals. Here, again, I should be in trouble with my readers, because readers never like a mob, for the simple reason that they can see a mob

49   E

any day in any city street. What they look for, and expect, are real people, such as, in an individual way, may come within their own lives and who, therefore, become interesting people.

If I did not, as I should not, be sure of my characters, I would develop them, as I should probably develop the plot, with much unnecessary detail, and that would finally confuse my readers and entirely bar the way to the success of my first novel.

There is an old story of the London book-world, which may be recalled as suggesting the things necessary in a first novel and a " first novelist." A well-known publisher, now no more, was called upon by the young son of an intimate friend with the question, " I want to be a novelist ; will you tell me, sir, what I should do ? "

" Young man," was the answer, " I cannot tell you how to succeed in the most difficult profession in the world. But I can give you one or two hints as to how to set about it. You should clearly decide in your mind what you wish to say ; then you should decide equally clearly how you wish to say it ; and finally you should say it all as clearly and concisely as you can in not any more than a hundred thousand words, and if you can make the words fewer, so much the better."

That was not only good advice to a young man self-called to be a novelist, but it was practically all the advice that can be given to anybody, young or old, who wishes to pursue the craft. There can be no general prescription for success, because the final deciding element is the presence or the absence of personality.

If there is no personality behind a story, it lacks life and colour and verity. It is merely a long stream of words which flow well or ill, but which bear on their bosom no living tale of human life such as a novel should carry. We do not all have personality, and perhaps it is as well that some of us should not have it. It is, however, a supreme gift, whether it amounts to talent or goes higher and becomes genius. This will appear from a glance at a few of the first novels which have been conspicuous in our time, especially as that also means a glance at their writers.

Some of you may not be old enough to recollect when ' The Stickit Minister,' by Mr. S. R. Crockett, came out and at once made a hit, not only in Scotland, where, for its colouring, it would naturally make a hit, but in England, in America, and wherever the English language is

spoken. Until then Mr. Crockett had been, as
he remained for some years, a Scots minister,
what the hero of his narrative would have been if
he had not have become " stickit." He was
only, however, the hero of one story in the book,
because it consisted of a series of tales.

The sketches appeared serially, from 1891
onwards, in the ' Christian Leader ' owned and
edited by Mr. William Howit Wylie, a master
of editorship. Mr. Crockett had the cuttings
from the ' Leader ' carefully pasted on to single
sheets of paper, edited, and made up in volume
form, and then he entrusted the finding of a
publisher to Mr. Pollock Wylie, who, after sub-
mitting the work to several leading London
houses, without result, managed to persuade his
friend, Mr. Fisher Unwin, to do a small edition.
It appeared in 1893, and its success was so great
that a second edition was instantly needed and
many other editions followed.

One might dwell on Sir James Barrie's ' Auld
Licht Idylls,' the first book to win him fame,
upon ' The Lightning Conductor,' by Mr. and
Mrs. C. N. Williamson, and upon many other
first novels which heralded success for their
writers. It is more interesting, however, because
less known ground, to speak of lesser and nearer

" first novelists," although probably that description would not apply to Miss Ethel M. Dell, who jumped into fame with ' The Way of an Eagle.'

It had appeared serially in a London magazine, and there its qualities of emotion and observation, and therefore of popularity, were noted by some onlooker who was not wrong. Why was it successful ? Perhaps the hero, Nick Radcliffe, had a considerable deal to do with that. He was not good looking, but heroes do not need to be good looking if they have hearts of gold, and he had one. He was a fascinating hero, if an ugly hero, and all the young folk took him to their favour and they have kept him there ever since, for ' The Way of an Eagle,' Miss Dell's first book has a continuing circulation.

Whenever you find a successful first novel, you find in it the touch of humanity and personality. It was present in ' David Harum,' an American first novel and " best seller," which was as successful here as it was across the Atlantic, because it was written under peculiar conditions. Its author, Mr. E. N. Westcott, had been a banker, and he became ill and the doctor said he would not live, and, being unable to work any more at banking, he sat down and wrote ' David Harum.'

It will be seen, therefore, that when he wrote it, he was a condemned man, that he was writing with his heart, his soul, and his mind working care-free of worldly things. It filled his illness to write the book, helped him through with it, but he could not find a publisher—anyhow not easily.

Eventually he threw the manuscript on to the top shelf of a cupboard, and there it lay until, as he said himself, he could " smell it whenever he opened the front door." Thanks to a happy chance, he did find a publisher, and on his advice he reconstructed the book ; and in its new shape it simply stormed to victory, only Westcott did not live long enough to be the happy " first novelist," he otherwise would have been.

" Ouida," the owner of many dogs which she treated better than she treated some of her friends, and Miss Braddon, her antithesis in appearance, character, and temperament, all wrote first novels of which one might say something. So did Thomas Hardy and George Meredith and Walter Besant and a whole string of Victorian writers, including Marion Crawford, whose ' Mr. Isaacs ' is a first novel to which one reader, at all events, constantly goes back, so attractive is it, so full of the colour, the romance, and the mystery of India.

Again, however, the younger novelists, those of to-day, claim us ; writers like Miss Sheila Kaye-Smith or Miss Victoria Sackville-West, who was a poetess until she became a novelist by writing ' Heritage.'

Her poetry was characterized by an unusual austerity of expression, combined with great mentality and descriptive power. When she wrote ' Heritage ' these gifts passed into wit, and the book was distinguished by a purity of style and a clarity of vision remarkable at a time when, perhaps, the finer qualities of literary craftsmanship are not cultivated by every English writer.

Somebody once asked Charles Reade the secret of story-telling, and he said : " Make 'em laugh, make 'em cry, make 'em wait." It has been well said that Mr. Denis Mackail carried out this ruling in his first novel, ' Bill the Bachelor,' and he carries it out in the books he has written since. He has humour, which makes you chuckle rather than guffaw, and this is a quality most precious to a novelist, because it gets the culti-vated reader as well as the other reader. It is easy to manage farce or low comedy—at all events, comparatively easy—but Mr. Mackail avoids those things, and makes his readers laugh as a jester would do, without putting out his tongue.

Not long ago there died a lady, Miss Lily Dougall, who won a name with a first story called 'The Zeitgeist.' She went on writing distinctive novels for a while, and then she turned to theology, and she published, in the year 1900, a work 'Pro Christo et Ecclesia,' which was much discussed and read in theological circles. Here was a case of a woman who could not only write good fiction, but admirable theology, as her subsequent books, including one entitled 'Christus Futurus,' proved beyond any shade of doubt.

Not every "first novelist" becomes a theologian, and one of Richard Cobden's daughters was content to be just a novelist after she had written 'Wistons,' with which Mr. Fisher Unwin led off his First Novel Library in 1902. The idea of that series was a recognition of the importance of the first novel, and Mr. G. K. Chesterton said cleverly that it showed "a very dark and cunning knowledge of human nature."

It was not as Ellen Millicent Cobden that Cobden's daughter wrote 'Wistons,' but as "Miles Amber." Her real name was not disclosed until her second novel, 'Sylvia Saxon,' came out, and she was very content to take her distinctions modestly and quietly, the only pity being that she did not write more, because she had a real gift, and it was something also to have a London publisher for a kinsman.

Did you happen, some years ago, to read a first novel, of unusual force and vigour, called 'The Mask,' by Mr. John Cournos? If you had asked about the author, you would have found that he was born near Kieff, in Russia, and that at the age of ten he emigrated with his family to Philadelphia. Quite rightly, we should associate the originality in the book with his early life story. There is no doubt that the experiences which meet a man in his young days, say from ten to twenty, bite deeper into the soul than the experiences of another time.

There is another new "first novelist," who should be noted, and her name, that of a Scotswoman, is Miss Agnes Mure McKenzie. Her novel had the title 'Without Conditions,' and the scenes of it were laid in the Aberdeenshire Highlands. Its austere beauty came from the lights and shades of that wonderful region, as they play on the lights and shades of the life of Janet Brodie, a very perfect Highland lady.

What Miss Mure McKenzie told was the love story of Janet Brodie and Alan Crawford, and it was the most beautiful thing in life to them both. He was a gallant gentleman, and she thought her love was returned, but alas, no ! That takes us to the heart of a tale as delicate as you could fancy, trembling a little on every page, yet strong with a strange, intense flame.

IX

OLD WINE IN NEW BOTTLES

IF you know London well you know Clifford's
Inn, which lies between Fetter Lane and
Chancery Lane, near by the old Temple Bar. It
cannot, having regard to this, be said to be
sequestered, but when you get within its gates
you do find an air of quiet.

Partly that comes from the aspect of age in
the buildings, and the worn trees which survive
with them, because the roar of traffic along
Fleet Street and the Strand is near and loud.
Partly it comes from the associations of the place,
because, somehow, a home of law creates an
atmosphere of settledness, of things ordered and
only to be done, and Clifford's Inn is in the
records with Lincoln's Inn and Gray's Inn, and
The Temple, though, as one might say, it has
long ceased " to practise."

Years ago, on a fine summer morning, I went
to Clifford's Inn seeking for somebody called

Samuel Butler, who had written a new book which excited curiosity. He had written other books earlier, but they had not all been much read, and so he was rather an unknown figure. He turned out to be in no want of advertisement for himself or his books, and really he never got it until he died. Then there came along quite a " boom " in ' Erewhon ' and its companion works, and as that " boom " has consolidated itself into a definite vogue, Samuel Butler is very well known to-day.

To me, anyhow, possibly because I talked with him in the flesh, he is a distinctive sign of the great business there has been, since the war, in old literature in new editions, a variation of the Scriptural phrase about new wine in old bottles. Nobody who pretends to be a serious reader should be outside this renaissance and persistence of authors who either belong to our time or to our generation. They are authors on the way to a permanent place in English literature, for a deal of testing is made of them by time and the public judgment, before they are awarded an eternal laurel wreath.

Samuel Butler's expression was one of amusement that anybody should be interested in him or what he did. He had made some money out of sheep in New Zealand, being a good farmer and looking like one, but he couldn't make authorship pay—not he. His ' Erewhon,' a fantasy of philosophy laid in a land of " Nowhere," was refused by George Meredith in his capacity as " reader " to a London publishing house. Well, there are many publishing houses which would like to have ' Erewhon ' now, and the ' Note-Books ' and the other writings of this Butler, so different a man from Bishop Butler.

" They told me," he said about his rejected ' Erewhon ' and Meredith, " he reported it was a philosophical work little likely to be popular with a large circle of readers. I hope that, if I had been their reader, and the book had been submitted to myself, I should have advised them to the same effect."

Probably ; and so probably would anybody, but the unexpected happens with books as in life, and ' Erewhon,' when it appeared in 1872, was a sound success. It was something new, something strange, and so if you want reading out of the ordinary, borrow it from the nearest library. Among Butler's books, it, at least, meets a test which he applied generally to authors. " If," he declared, " a writer, a painter, or a musician makes me feel that he held those things to be lovable which I myself hold to be lovable, I am satisfied ; art is only interesting in so far as it reveals the personality of the artist."

Surely that is the proof of all writing, as far, certainly, as the mass of people are concerned ; that in it, as a medium of communication, we meet some one, or some characters whom, if we could, we would like to meet personally. It will have occurred to you that when you sit down by the fire of an evening, with a favourite book in your hand, you are really sitting hand in hand with a beloved friend. It is always the human touch, however it may be expressed in language, which grips us, because it is life speaking to life.

Another characteristic Englishman, W. H. Hudson, resembled Samuel Butler in the one thing that to him also high fame came late. But it did come in time for him to know it, and indeed when, in his later years, his writings began to bring in enough for a simple sustenance, he gave up a modest Civil List pension which he had enjoyed. A man who did that must, the veriest stranger to him would reason, be worth reading, for it is hard, human nature being what it is, to put away something useful which we have only to let alone and it will stay with us.

Hudson was a modest, gentle, retiring gentleman, who loved Nature in all her moods, and knew most of them. He communed with her and with himself in South America, in England, and elsewhere, and out of this communing sprang his books, of all of which there are now reasonably priced editions. No, not all, for he wrote a novel under another name, and its rarity may be gathered from the fact that a copy of the first edition has fetched seventy-one pounds in a London sale-room.

It was a specially interesting first edition, because it had been Hudson's own copy, presented to him by " H. H." He was " Henry Harford," the pen-name used for the novel by its writer. The story was called ' Fan,' a young girl was the heroine of it, and it appeared in print in 1892. May be, although one does not know, it may have been published " on commission " as the term is, and the terms are, when the writer of a book is himself responsible for the venture. Anyhow, the edition was a small one of only three hundred and fifty copies, which fact makes a surviving one, if you can lay hands on it anywhere, all the more valuable.

We owe a tremendous debt to Englishmen

who have gone forth into the world and done things before sitting down to write. One does not mean mere chroniclers of an individual journey, or a special enterprise. One means men who found the mine of genuine authorship and literature in their own experiences, men like Hudson and Joseph Conrad. " Ah ! " you will explain ; " but Conrad was born a Pole." True, but that makes no difference to the argument, and, indeed, it might be said to strengthen it, because a line of literature which gathers to itself a talent like Conrad's must be fine mettle in our English pasture.

What must he, routing round his very English farm near Canterbury, in Kent, have thought about the sale, for over a thousand pounds, of the manuscript of his early story, ' Almayer's Folly ' ? It would have recalled to him his experiences with the publishers, until it became dog-eared and worn-looking. Possibly he grew a little despondent about finding an Appian Way in literature. But unconsciously, while he sailed the seas as an officer of our mercantile marine, he stored his mind with the rough treasure stuff which later he was to mint into novels already classed A1.

If you have not read them, and if you think

you would like to try them—for, mind you, they need reading, not mere skipping through—why not begin with ' The Nigger of the Narcissus.' One advises that because Conrad himself has written, " It is the story by which, as a creative artist, I stand or fall, and which, at all events, no one else could have written. A landmark of literature, I can safely say, for nothing like it has ever been written before."

Here there comes in a curious little point touching the MS. of ' The Nigger of the Narcissus,' which Conrad began writing in Brittany when he was on his honeymoon, and which was finished within a year. " I intended," he has said about this manuscript, " to keep it by me, and then leave it to the manuscript department of the British Museum. They preserve many less significant manuscripts there," he added, thinking of the significance of the novel in his own literary development. Somehow it got to America, unlike another Conrad manuscript which came to grief on the way.

This was ' Kerin,' a short piece of work that went down, as did W. T. Stead, and a whole company of people, on the ill-fated *Titanic*. When a tangle, pleasant or unpleasant, begins, it is apt to increase its coils, and, strangely enough,

A LONDON BOOK WINDOW

Captain Joseph Conrad was one of the sailor-men called in for the *Titanic* inquiry. Nay, there is a manuscript by him in which he wrote about ' Some Aspects of the English *Titanic* Inquiry,' with the full literary quality you will find in his novels. That quality owes something to the inspiration of English poetry, for Conrad knew it well and loved it well, as when, for his ' Rover ' he quoted the lines of Spenser :

"Sleep after toyle, port after stormie seas,
  Ease after warre, death after life, does greatly please."

Old wine in new bottles ! It has, in a literary way, been flowing freely, and if it has found its way to the hearts of a fresh generation of readers, so much the better. There has been a great to do about Herman Melville, the American writer whom, a year or so ago, a few English critics thought they had " discovered " for England. Nothing of the sort. His ' Typee ' and his ' Omoo ' of the Southern Seas are as intimate to some of us as the memories of our childhood. It was his whaling story and autobiography, ' Moby Dick,' that caused the belated shouting, but it also was familiar to English readers, and perhaps less good than ' Typee.'

Some day some confident literary fellow will

happen on Dana's ' Two Years Before the Mast,' and he will exclaim, " Here's the finest sea book ever written." He will not be far wrong, because that has been understood for half a century. Even so, the clever itch of not very widely-read critics is good, in that it directs others to treasure pages lying in wait for them. Nobody can have failed to read ' Robinson Crusoe,' but there are other books by Defoe worthy of consultation, and the current reprinting of these, although in limited editions, has been so much literary service to the community.

A much nearer person, Anthony Trollope, has come along again with his Barsetshire novels of a Victorian England which has almost passed away. He has been made welcome, a little out of curiosity about himself, for he could write at the rate of a thousand words an hour, and he made nearly seventy thousand pounds, and also a little out of curiosity about the England which he describes. Anthony had no genius, and perhaps prided himself on the fact, but he took uncommon trouble to build stories of plot and character, and he is worth looking up in the new editions of him.

George Borrow we have always with us, may be, to some people, for that wonderfully described

fight with the tinker in 'Lavengro.' Ever so
many quiet folk are pugilistic enough to like to
read about a round, so long as nobody comes to
any great harm. Borrow may be said to have
carried the Bible in one hand—think of his
'Bible in Spain'—and vagabondage in the
other, and the two missions keep his memory
green.

Another old favourite in constant new clothes
is Jane Austen, whose reticence of style often
hides much good thought. Even Mrs. Monta-
gue, the Queen of the Blue Stockings, has been
looking up, and a very different, much more
romantic and more recent writer, Robert Louis
Stevenson, is blowing in new collected editions.
They follow the Vailima, the Pentland, the Swan-
ston and the Edinburgh editions of his writings,
and all of them go up in value with the keeping,
like good wine in good bottles ; so, clearly, they
pay the buyer a double debt, like the bedstead
in Goldsmith's 'Deserted Village.'

Finally, if you visit a sufficient bookshop you
will find on its counters that John Morley and
Thomas Hardy are old wine in new bottle men,
meaning that they are in recent collected editions.
Between Morley as an essayist, and Hardy as a
novelist, you are sure of as good writing as has

been done in English, within memory, and with a comforting knowledge like that, one can fitly bring to a close this calling back of a book world of yesterday.

X

ABOUT PUBLISHERS' READERS

YOU probably have a turn for books, even, it may be, a real gift for understanding what a book should be and how to make it a book. In that case, what would you think of being a " publishers' reader " ?

What is that ? you may ask, because it is possible to be quite " booky," even very well informed about English literature, new and old, and yet never to have heard the name and office of a " publishers' reader," for they only apply to a limited band.

It does not mean what a young man, perhaps a rather foolish young man, thought when he heard it used by a well-known London publisher. " Oh," said he, " if you can't get people to read your books, send them to me as they come out, because I have lots of spare time. It would be so kind of you ! "

A " publishers' reader " is something very

different from that, as you will understand, when I tell you that John, Viscount Morley was one. He began with Daniel and Alexander Macmillan, the founders of the Macmillan house, and he was an active " reader " for a quarter of a century. Within that time he would have seen in manuscript, or heard about, every important book that came their way. Even to the end, when he was a very old man, but as keen as ever mentally, he and Sir Frederick Macmillan, now the head of this great hostel of literature, talked books, for they were true friends.

We are, by taking John Morley's case, a very illustrious case, instructed in what is meant by the term " publishers' reader." He was far more than that to the Macmillans, because he was their chief adviser and a counsellor of ' Macmillan's Magazine,' now, alas, no more, for the rather literary magazine has given place to the very popular magazine, though ' Blackwood's,' ' Chambers's ' and ' Cornhill ' all happily survive.

Every " publishers' reader " may not be chief literary adviser to the firm with which he is associated, as the job, if one may use that very plain but always expressive word, varies a good deal. There is the " reader " who, we shall say, is retained on the premises, which means, in effect, that he handles manuscripts in the first degree. But, radiating around him, although they may not come to the office, will be other "readers" to whom manuscripts are sent constantly, and special "readers" with a high knowledge of their own subjects, to whom manuscripts go occasionally.

You can, therefore, in a small way, be a "publishers' reader" without having to work in his office, but Mr. G. K. Chesterton did that when he was beginning his fragrant and fruitful career as a man of letters. He was, for a time, in the office of Mr. Fisher Unwin, who has had a faculty for enlisting talent before it was recognized elsewhere. Mr. Edward Garnett was a literary pillar to him, and so was Mr. W. H. Chesson, both of them sons of notable men. It was Mr. W. H. Chesson who first found the literary gold in Joseph Conrad's 'Almayer's Folly,' a circumstance which suggests what we may owe to the "publishers' reader."

He has been called a "literary taster," but that description is not very good, because it does not cover all that he has to do. True, his first question, when a manuscript is in his hands, will be, "Is this good work, and does it have anything to say to literature?" But that is a high-road which is not often present, and so he has to ask

himself, " Is this interesting, and will it sell ? "
Probably he finds himself embarked on a middle
course, which he expresses in the self-communing,
" Yes, there's good stuff here, only the book must
be recast, in large part re-written, and will the
author be agreeable ? "

One always likens a publishing house to a newspaper office, in that both have staffs whose business it is to winnow reading for the public, in one
case news reading, in the other case book reading.
Similar gifts are needed by those who do this
work ; intuition for what is human and appealing,
critical knowledge, such as puts a thing, whether
news or literature, in its right perspective.
Neither calling, that of the newspaper man or
that of the publishing man, is easy, for the supply
of material is enormous, the amount of it that
can go into print very small. Some London publisher has been saying that within two particular
months he received a hundred novels for con-
sideration, and that only one of them was worthy
of being made into a book.

John Morley edited the " English Men of
Letters Series " for the Macmillans, and it contains volumes like Dean Church's ' Bacon,' Dr.
Saintsbury's ' Dryden,' and Mr. Augustine Birrell's ' Hazlitt,' so we may gather the fineness of

73

his editorship. But it has come to be understood that when John Richard Green's ' Short History of the English People' was put before him, he was not greatly impressed with it. At all events he was doubtful how far it would succeed, but it succeeded instantly, and to-day, in several forms, it pursues its successful way as an admirable and readable story of the English people, in contrast with a mere story of their kings and rulers, such as, in the past, has frequently come from writers less democratic than Green.

Even a " publishers' reader," whether the great author who was that in other days, or the smaller man of letters who mostly is that to-day, cannot be always wise, always right. He makes hits, and he misses, and that is the way of human life, and we should just be thankful if, when the score comes to be counted up, we have made a good average over the space of our activities.

George Meredith was " reader " to Chapman and Hall, who originally published various of his books, as earlier they were the publishers of Charles Dickens. Thus it was that one of Mr. Thomas Hardy's first ventures in fiction came under the notice of Meredith, who helped his friend by encouraging him, although, indeed, he was predestined to his high place. All the way

74

from South Africa there came, eventually to Meredith's desk, a manuscript entitled 'The Story of an African Farm,' with the name "Ralph Iron" on the title-page, and that was the beginning of Olive Schreiner's fame.

Andrew Lang, "Andra' wi' the brindled hair" of his friend Stevenson, read for the Longmans and wrote at "The Sign of the Ship" in their magazine. The association gave young England the Blue Fairy Books, and other books of the same kind, which young England is still liking. When he could, Lang read his manuscripts at St. Andrew's, to which he was devoted, but London was also agreeable to him, and he was a distinctive and valued figure at the Savile Club.

Here is a little personal story which illustrates his personality, for a story will often be more effective than a chapter of the Bible in the way of revealing. He had a London house in a pleasant street at the far end of that dull, seemingly endless thoroughfare, Cromwell Road. He was inviting some one to dinner, and being asked, "How do I get to you?" he answered, "You walk and walk and walk along Cromwell Road, and when you drop down exhausted, I'll come out of my house and take you in—to dinner!"

James Payn, the novelist, read for Smith, Elder

and Company, a publishing house of much enterprise and interest, which was merged in that of
the Murrays when Mr. Reginald Smith died,
during the war. No writer of quality, talent or
genius, is ever really " discovered," because he or
she will arrive somehow, somewhere, somewhen.
But young writers, when they come knocking,
can be heartily bidden " Come in," and probably
James Payn had that hospitality for " Seton
Merriman," whose real name was Scott, for Stanley Weyman, for the witty author of ' Vice Versa,'
and for more of their quality.

Ever since William Heinemann " commenced
publisher " in Bedford Street, Strand, London,
Mr. Edmund Gosse, a veteran but still active
Victorian, has been associated with the trade-
mark of the Windmill. It was chosen by Heinemann to embellish the title-pages of his books,
and not a few of those books have come through
the ripe counsel of Mr. Gosse. Mostly, perhaps,
his activities have had to do with *belles lettres*,
anyhow not with fiction, although one could bet
that he is a confirmed novel reader in the ordinary
sense. Nor is it at all unlikely that he may have
been " part and parcel " in the finding of those
long, literary, very Victorian novels by William
de Morgan, which gave us all so much pleasure.

ABOUT PUBLISHERS' READERS

Mr. John Murray, following a tradition of his house, has always, in a way, been his own " reader " ; that is to say, he would make himself acquainted with a manuscript, know all about it, have a direct say in its acceptance or refusal. Nobody, perhaps, could command a larger circle of literary advisers, and have not successive editors of the ' Quarterly Review ' been a school of literature in themselves ? Recent editors have been Lord Ernle, when he was Mr. Rowland Prothero, and his brother, the late Sir George Prothero. Now Mr. John Murray himself, and Mr. C. E. Lawrence, who is well known as a novelist, are joint editors of the ' Quarterly,' a happy arrangement.

The Blackwoods have always been closely identified with their magazine, called familiarly " Maga," and also with their books. They gave us Mrs. Katherine Cecil Thurston's detective story of political life, for one might almost call it that, ' John Chilcote, M.P.' They captured ' With Kitchener to Khartoum,' a brilliant narrative of a little war, by G. W. Stevens, a special correspondent for whom Lord Northcliffe had a real affection. They have always had a strong military side, probably because one Blackwood marched to Kandahar with Lord Roberts, and it was in ' Blackwood's ' that we made acquaintance with " Linesman's " vivid sketches of the South African war. The " family reader," new model, may be a very effective method of " reading " when good books are in question.

It was Mr. Arrowsmith, of Bristol, a shrewd bookseller become publisher, who found Hugh Conway's ' Called Back ' and ' Dark Days.' It was Andrew Chatto who bought outright, as publishers once did, but rarely can do now, thanks to the vigilant literary agent, Thomas Hardy's ' Under the Greenwood Tree,' and Hall Caine's ' Deemster.' There are a dozen ways of " reading " for a publisher, but mainly there is the old-fashioned way, which sought genius, talent, quality and only shouted when it came on one of the three, and the new-fashioned way, in which a new-fashioned publisher will say casually, sweetly, over the office cup of tea, " We don't seem to have happened on anything that sells, not recently, have we ? "

It is really a question of two English publics, for that of a quarter of a century ago was educated, cultured, limited, while that of to-day is eager, omnivorous, unlimited. The old reader was negative, like the old journalist ; that is, he took what he thought was best and sent the rest back with his thanks and compliments. The new reader is formative, that is, he will suggest books to authors as well as select from manuscripts come along by chance. The old fellow was solid and cautious, reliable, while the new fellow is sure of himself, willing to take a literary gamble within measure. The ultimate end will be the same in both cases, meaning that time and public opinion will decide when a book is a book, or only something made to look like one.

But no book nowadays, or else the publisher concerned is foolish and no gentleman, is dismissed to its author with the enclosure : " Our reader reports unfavourably on your manuscript, and therefore we can only return it with apologies for having kept it so long." Reasons for its return will be given, and often they are entirely apart from itself, as, for instance, that it is not the particular kind of book published by a particular house, that it is not long enough, or that it is too long, because you never know what a manuscript may be up against.

Every publisher has his associations, which he has cultivated, or which have grown round him, as love thrives on propinquity. Mr. E. V. Lucas is a leading literary spirit with Methuen, and he is also a member of the ' Punch ' staff. Probably that is why, if you are looking for a book by a ' Punch ' man, you are more likely to find it in Methuen's list than in any other list.

Mr. Frank Swinnerton, the novelist, was alive enough when he gathered in the manuscript of ' The Young Visiters ' for Chatto. It was shown to him in a friendly way, and he recognized a " find," so there is luck in " reading," as in everything else. That is what some people would say, but, of course, all luck consists in grasping fortune when it comes, instead of letting it pass in the night.

No " publishers' reader " of to-day has done better work, perhaps, than Mr. Newmann Flower, of Cassell's in La Belle Sauvage Yard, where, anciently, the coaches started and arrived. He is the modern editor-reader at his best, a man whose knowledge guides his *flair*, whose bravery of mind is equalled by his modesty of heart, who knows more of Handel than anybody in England, and who, with the joys of music, chases the worries of " reading " away, but never, never a good writer or a likely book.

One would have liked Sir William Robertson Nicoll to write the study, with examples, which he alone could have written of the " publishers' reader." He was one of the masters of the calling, as behold the publishing house of Hodder and Stoughton, which his literary gifts did much to build up, including the " discovery," in company with James Greenwood, of the only Barrie, a new "Wizard of the North."

XI

LIVES OF GREAT MEN

EVERY book has a history before we see it, certainly every notable book, just as a child lives before it is born. Nothing that is created takes being instantly, for creation, with its poetic mystery and beauty, is the nearest we get to divinity.

You remember reading, in ' Uncle Tom's Cabin,' about Topsy who " jes' grow'd." It was a wise saying, lightly said, for nearly everything that matters just grows and cannot be forced along by artificial measures. Thus it is that the journals and magazines which climb to real influence and deep-rooted prosperity, are mostly those which spring modestly from a root of personality, not from mere money power.

With such thoughts as " preface," for always we speak of books, may I tell you, perhaps from unusual inside knowledge, the story of the two most notable political biographies of our time, that of Gladstone and that of Beaconsfield. The curious thing is that, though they are so recent, they take pride of place among all our English political memoirs.

What had we in the way of authorized official memoirs about Pitt or Chatham, Fox or Burke, Peel or Palmerston ? Nothing that took classic rank, and only with the passage of years, and in independent, detached studies, did those figures of English public life come into their due. We have had John Morley's ' Burke ' and Sir George Otto Trevelyan's ' Fox,' and Lord Rosebery's brilliant ' Pitt,' and other monographs, which will readily occur to the well-read man. They made up, in a measure, and that was all, for the absence of any English political biographies comparable in interest with literary memoirs like Boswell's ' Johnson,' or Lockhart's ' Scott,' or Trevelyan's ' Macaulay.'

But now we have a ' Gladstone ' and a ' Beaconsfield,' both works of the first importance, having regard alike to the long parts played in English history by their heroes, and by reason of their literary quality. No doubt this quality is richest in the ' Gladstone,' for was not its author one of the modern masters of English, and moreover he had a more varied and therefore a richer personality for his subject. But both books definitely remedy what had been a grave defect of English political biography on the former model, its sacrifice of style and form, colour and character, to mere material.

You can almost hear the old biographers saying to themselves : " Here's lots of stuff, papers, letters, diaries ! Pile them together, fling them to the printer, and let him do what he likes with them." It was not quite so bad as that, but generally what an old-time student got was a mass of raw records through which he had to wade as best he could, instead of those records crushed into a living portrait. There we were far behind the French political memoir, which always sought the soul of a man or a woman, though, as a whole, our literature is, perhaps, richer in biography, as it is in poetry, than that of France.

" Be inspired," Gladstone once said, " with the belief that life is a great and honourable calling, not a mean and grovelling thing that we are to struggle through as best we can. . . ." If he saw life on that noble plane, it was fitting that his own should be written on the same plane, and it was.

However you regard him, he lived an epic, and clearly there was nobody who could express it so

simply, so sincerely, so knowledgeably, as his
dear friend and colleague John Morley. " J.
Morley," he wrote somewhere in the diary he
kept, " is, on the whole, about the best stay I
have," and it was true posthumously as well as
in the political fray. Hero and author, between
them, went to the making of a book which would
still have been irresistible even if it had not, in
the broad sense, been an authoritative political
history of modern England.

But what were John Morley's feelings when,
having accepted the call of the Gladstone family
to write the book, he went to Hawarden to survey
the materials for it ? He probably wished himself back in his own quiet, ordered London study,
where everything was familiar, because he was
confronted with an untold treasury of Gladston-
ianæ which he had to rifle for the essentials. It
was a task that only a brave man of letters, giving
up years in self-sacrifice, could face, and John
Morley did that and triumphed.

To him writing was always an affair of the
recluse, something that called him away from the
world, an art which he could only follow, as he
only would follow it, in solitude. When, with
two helpers, he had mastered Gladstone's moun-
tain of literary remains, he sat down at his desk

every morning, except Sunday, at nine o'clock. He went on all the day writing, writing, writing, sometimes slowly, sometimes rapidly, always with his severe test of quality anchored beside him. He wrote with his own hand the whole of the ' Gladstone,' except the absolute letters and quotations given in it, and if you would like to know what that means, get the book and count its words.

Your task would be spoiled if I were to tell you roughly how many there are, and that would be a pity. No wonder there is a charming story which tells just how John Morley felt when, at the end of three years of a literary toil, rare in any annals, he finished the ' Gladstone.' He was asked by a friend over Andrew Carnegie's hospitable table at Skibo Castle, in Scotland : " Aren't you glad it's done ? " And he answered : " Yes, I'm very glad and—very lonely ! "

He had his reward, as most worthy tasks, undertaken with a single heart, are rewarded, for the biography, in its three handsome, red-clothed volumes, was a far-flung success. Everybody read it, and within a few years of its publication it had sold 117,000 sets, representing 271,000 volumes in the English and American editions, and people had spent over £100,000 in its purchase.

LIVES OF GREAT MEN

Sad is the story of good books which have failed to find their readers and their fame, but there could hardly be a more exalted joy than to write a good book and have the world seal it so. Why did the 'Gladstone' succeed so highly? Why does it remain, as it always will remain, a very living book? Because it tells the life-story of the biggest personality England has known for long, because of the affectionate hold he had upon the hearts of the people, because of his wide range of interests, from politics to theology, from poetry to finance, whereby he touched every book-reader somewhere, and finally, because John, Viscount Morley, himself a first-class states-man and more than a first-class writer, was the biographer.

What is the moral behind this, for a moral should always be drawn when, for certain, it can be found. The moral is that the world, which is equally full of curiosity and sympathy, the desire to understand and the wish to do honour, will always respond to " the great thing which a great man may make of life."

That is a Morleyism, and the 'Gladstone' is full of lovely thoughts set in simple, beautiful language. Such is the language which wins those who like style as well as the man, but equally,

if without consciousness on his part, it wins the
" man in the street." He reads with his heart as
much as with his head, and it is this, no doubt,
that keeps him wise in his choice of books, for
does not Robert Burns, who knew the " man in
the street," long before the phrase had been
coined, tell us : " The heart's aye the part aye,
that makes us right or wrong."

It was a Welsh miner, poor but ardent in reading, who, when he finally managed to buy the
cheap ' Gladstone,' wrote : " Once I had the loan
of the original edition over the Sunday from a
library, and I devoured it for forty-eight hours
without a stop." That incident touches the
heart, and a test of the pocket, less winning though
it be, will also betoken the achievement of the
' Gladstone.'

One day in March, 1856, the Longmans sent
Macaulay a cheque for £20,000 on account of
the profits of the third and fourth volumes of his
' History of England.' This has been the record
book-cheque of the English literary world, but
if the royalties, paid by the Macmillans to the
Gladstone family, on the ' Gladstone,' were expressed together, they would make a far larger
cheque than Macaulay's. When one says that,
one adds in explanation that the rights of the

biography belong to Gladstone's family, who gave John Morley £10,000 for writing it, and later a second recognition and thanks-offering of £3,000.

We do not have such full details, literary and material, of the ' Beaconsfield,' as have been set down around the ' Gladstone,' partly because the stories of the two books are so different. All the conditions were right for the almost immediate on-going of the one book, while the other was held up in a most disconcerting way. The consequence was that the ' Gladstone ' came out, as it were, with a bang, while he was fresh in the minds of a generation to whom he had been the Grand Old Man. On the other hand the ' Beaconsfield ' drifted unwritten over the years, until those who knew him in life had passed away or grown old, for he died, at his beloved Hughenden, in Buckinghamshire, on April 19, 1881, and the last volumes of the biography have only recently appeared.

Somebody has said, wittily and therefore not necessarily truly, that he left all his papers to his famous friend and secretary, " Monty " Corry, Lord Rowton, because, in such safe keeping, they were pretty certain never to be published. Certainly he could not have done that, because do we

not find him writing in ' Contarini Fleming ' :
" Read no history, nothing but biography, for
that is life without theory."

" Monty " Corry, whose entitled name chris-
tened Rowton House, which he founded, was not
in any manner a literary man, and " Dizzy "
could hardly have expected him to do the biography. Simply he was left all the papers to
handle as he judged well towards a biography,
only those concerning public affairs were not to
be drawn upon without the consent of the
Sovereign. Here comes in the gain which time
gives a book in fullness of material, as against
its loss in the passing of the contemporary
generation, and the two ways are admirably
illustrated by the ' Beaconsfield ' and the
' Gladstone.'

What Lord Rowton did was to arrange " Dizzy's " papers, or have them arranged, but the
years flew, and the question, keenly discussed
from time to time, remained : " Who's to write
the Life ? " A well-known London conservative
journalist, the late Mr. T. E. Kebble, was mentioned, because he had been on very friendly
terms with Disraeli. Other likely biographers
were thought to be Lord Rosebery and George
Wyndham, both admirers of Benjamin as a cha-

racter and both brilliant writers, as their books amply assure us.

Nothing, however, had happened when Lord Rowton died in 1903, and all the papers then passed to the Beaconsfield Trustees, the late Lord Rothschild, the late Mr. Leopold Rothschild and Sir Philip Rose, who succeeded his father, " Dizzy's " friend and lawyer, as one of the executors. " We must do something," said Lord Rothschild, who was the active trustee, and one morning he asked Mr. Moberley Bell, well known as the then manager of ' The Times,' to find the right biographer and have the Life written and published. He, in turn, invited Mr. W. F. Moneypenny, a tried member of ' The Times ' staff, to undertake the work, and eventually the invitation was accepted. Mr. Moneypenny, whose health was not strong, died after getting out two volumes, and he left the basis of a chapter on ' Tancred ' for a third volume.

It happened that Mr. George Earle Buckle, at that time, and for long, editor of ' The Times,' had, as an advising friend, read Mr. Money-penny's volumes in proof, and so knew about the whole business from the inside. When, therefore, he resigned the editorship of ' The Times ' he had the leisure and the will to complete

Mr. Moneypenny's biographical task, and he did so with great ability and warm acceptance.

All together the 'Beaconsfield' has run to six volumes, or twice the number of the 'Gladstone,' though that circumstance does not certify the actual difference of length in the books. "Dizzy" reaches the crown of his career in the last two volumes, for they tell of the famous purchase of the Suez Canal shares, and of his return from Berlin saying he bore "Peace with honour." They also include, what only became available at the last moment, a budget of letters written by "Dizzy," after his wife died, to an English lady of quality. He was a man of sentiment, and those exquisite and curious letters continue and complete his sentimental journey. It took in Mrs. Brydges Willyams, before and after he married her, and there are epistles which tell that, in his great gallantry, he did not exclude Queen Victoria. But then "Dizzy" knew that half the intellect of the world and three-quarters of its heart are really the jewels of womanhood.

XII

BYRON AND THE MURRAYS

WOULD you like to go with me, I in memory, you in fancy, to a literary shrine of London which everybody does not see, though Mr. John Murray is courtesy itself to the serious pilgrim ?

It is the drawing-room of his house in Albemarle Street, by Piccadilly, a place full of memories and associations, with Byron as the centre of them, and he is one of the few English poets who won a European fame at a stride. It was at Number Eight, St. James's Street, down the hill towards St. James's Palace, that he awoke one morning to find himself famous ; but to be intimate with this fame we must go to the home of the Murrays in Albemarle Street.

You like the thought ! Small wonder if you do, for in this drawing-room, which the human traffic of London passes without a salute, Byron's journals were burned, so ending, in kindly smoke,

93

a document of a romance and an adventure, of a passion and a glowing prose, that the world would have lingered on to-day, not, perhaps, always to the exaltation of Byron's good name. You can, in imagination, almost hear its notes of poetry singing up the chimney, now cool in its white marble fireplace, to a blaze that was both historic and generous. It is a long room and high in the ceiling, as the old London way was, but you hardly notice a detail like this because it is so full of Byron treasures which arrest the eye and capture the mind.

The Murray drawing-room is also notable because Byron and Scott first met here on a date of April in the year of Waterloo, 1815. They came together under the wing of their mutual friend John Murray II., who has sometimes been called Byron's Murray. You may, in his journals, find the record : " On this day I introduced Lord Byron and Sir Walter Scott, and they remained for nearly two hours talking to each other." There is even a tradition that they limped downstairs arm in arm, supporting each other, and that is likely enough, for they were both lame men. A story goes, and it may not deserve to go far, that, in a recent year, an American walked into the Murray publishing office, next door to the house, gazed raptly at a twisty iron stair which, for trade uses, connects its floors, remarked, " So that is the stair ! " and was gone before anybody could say him nay.

We know it is another stair, an easier and more beautiful one, which we climb to the room of the Murray treasures. Glance around, and you find portraits of Byron, Coleridge, Lockhart, Sir Walter Scott's son-in-law, Moore, Campbell, and other literary worthies who were associated with the Murrays. Byron was not only a dandy, but a " sport," and a draught screen which you will examine with curiosity is here, a queer testimony to his " sportsmanship."

It was bought by John Murray II. when Byron's effects were sold up to pay his debts, or some of them, for the " Gay Gordon " in him took care that he should never be out of debt. He had the screen made by Gentleman Jackson, who was his trainer, but why he should have set him to such a job there is no explanation. Anyhow, on one side of it there are portraits of the pugilists of Byron's day, Dan Mendoza, Jack Broughton, George Stevenson, Molineux, Pearce, Jackson himself, and the rest of the gang ; and on the other side pictures of leading actors and actresses, also of the Byronic time.

But Mr. John Murray, John the Fourth, will show you something else with a finer and more intimate touch of the poet ; Byron's snuff-box, containing a lock of his hair, still brown and shot with gold. You handle this box tenderly, for here, indeed, you are in immediate contact with a genius who will last all down the world. Byron is brought very near, too, by a little bottle containing hemlock which he sent from Athens to Albemarle Street, where it finds a faithful wardenship. He described it as the direct descendant of the hemlock with which Socrates was poisoned. A paper enwrapping the mouth of the bottle is bleached by time, and so is its fragment of writing by Byron. Even so, you can read that " The hemlock contained in this phial was gathered for, and by, me at Athens, Feb. 1811 Bn "—short for Byron.

More precious still is a Bible, bound in red Morocco, which you are shown, because it was Byron's Bible. There is, you must know, an old tale to the effect that Byron, at some thoughtless or angry moment, for he had temper and he could forget favours, sent John Murray II. a Bible wherein he had changed a well-known passage to read : " Now Barabbas was a publisher."

Well, Byron's Bible is before you, and you will
see that there is no written mark whatever, nothing, on the page where the Barabbas passage
occurs, or, indeed, anywhere else. The tale had no
shadow of fact, so far as Byron and the Murrays
were concerned, and let that be definite, for a
picturesque lie is hard to kill. If any incident of
the sort belongs to the English book-world, and
perhaps there was a real version, it has no concern
with Byron and John Murray II., whose friendship was of a perfect quality.

Out of it comes a copy of Byron's ' English
Bards and Scotch Reviewers,' on the fly-leaf of
which he made a notable confession. " The binding of this volume," he put down, " is consider-
ably too valuable for its contents. Nothing but
its being the property of another prevents me
from consigning this miserable record of mis-
placed anger and indiscriminate acrimony to the
flames."

A second copy of the ' English Bards and
Scotch Reviewers,' which had personally been
Byron's, is also among the Murray relics, and it
bears an apology dated July 14, 1816, on the
same matter : " The greater part of this satire,"
you read, " I most sincerely wish had never been
written, not only on account of the injustice of

much of the critical, and some of the personal part of it, but the tone and temper are such as I cannot approve."

Need it be said that there we have side-lights on the attack which Byron, smarting from criticism by the ' Edinburgh Review ' set, and blaming some of it to Scott, made on him in his ' English Bards and Scotch Reviewers.' If you will look up your ' Byron,' you will come upon this hurt and hurting passage :

" And think'st thou, Scott, by vain conceit, perchance,
  On public taste to foist thy stale romance,
  Though Murray, with his Millar, may combine,
  To yield thy muse just half-a-crown a line."

A footnote to those lines of literary history is that the Millar mentioned was the publisher whom John Murray II. succeeded, when he moved to Albemarle Street from newspaper Fleet Street, where the first Murray of all commenced business. The comment on the lines, and on Byron's retractation of them, is that from the moment he met Scott, in the Murray drawing-room, remember, he conceived a warm admiration for him. It should, then, be clear that John Murray II., in that he found the opportunity, was the begetter of a friendship which came to adorn English literature.

BYRON AND THE MURRAYS

How well it regards Byron, we see in the fact that no manuscript of any value by him has ever come into the market. The Murray possessions, in the way of manuscripts and letters, are priceless, and a figure will never be put on them. It is something to own the MSS. of Scott's ' Abbot,' to have manuscripts by Queen Victoria, Peel, Gladstone, and many a celebrity besides. It is much to have a First Folio Shakespeare, an original copy of the Edinburgh Edition of Burns, and other such trophies. But the supreme pride of the House of Murray is its Byron manuscripts and letters which were the making of the Definitive Byron published some twenty years ago.

A big safe swings open to your wondering gaze, for within it are a dozen pigeon-holes crammed with Byron literary remains. Here are manuscripts he wrote, proofs he corrected, endless epistles in his bold, hurrying hand. Note, in particular, two bulky packets, one rich with the letters of Byron to John Murray II., between the years 1811 and 1824, the other freighted with Murray's letters to Byron, for, in those days, correspondence was an art, not merely a business.

How privileged one is to handle the large sheets

of paper on which Byron wrote ' Childe Harold,'
especially as they directly recall an incident wherein Gladstone and Browning had a part. Browning charged Byron with bad grammar, and in
proof of it quoted the line from ' Childe Harold ' :
" And dashest him to earth—there let him lay."
Said Gladstone, a keen admirer of the poet, if not
the man : " Byron seems to me to have used the
language always as a master, but sometimes as a
tyrant." His use of " lay," Gladstone put among
the tyrannies, but he pointed out that Sterne in
the ' Sentimental Journey' kept him company,
a " twin error, not an excuse." As for Byron,
one observes that he wrote " lay " with especial
clearness, so showing that he was using it after
reflection.

At times his " copy," as we may call the manuscript of even a great poet, was very difficult to
read, and he corrected much. If he was in England he called for proof after proof, and each
would carry changes back to the printer. When
he was abroad he would send new manuscripts,
with instructions for their urgent publication.
This kind of thing gave good opportunities for
such a misprint as is associated with the 182nd
stanza of ' Childe Harold,' where the famous lines
occur :

BYRON AND THE MURRAYS

"Thy shores are empires, changed in all save thee—
Assyria, Greece, Rome, Carthage, what are they?
Thy waters washed them power while they were free."

Now in several successive editions of ' Childe
Harold' "washed them power" was printed
"wasted then," and thus the true rendering of
the last line was lost, thanks to the apparent maze
of Byron's heavily scored manuscript. It was
he, himself, who discovered the misprint and, in
a letter from Greece, called attention to it. But
somehow it was not corrected until years after his
death, and if you have the fortune to own an early
edition of ' Childe Harold' you can still read the
mistake there.

It is a very wonderful feeling which one has
in the Murray drawing-room, with the spirit of
Byron so close, and so many other British men
of literary genius in the atmosphere. Think of
William Gifford, the famous editor of the ' Quarterly,' whom Byron called, with every reason, his
" grand patron " and his " Magnus Apollo."
Probably he valued Gifford and Scott most
among all his writing friends, and he had a
genius for friendship when he liked.

Beside them, no doubt, ranked John Murray
II., of whom and the poet, John Murray IV. once
said to me : " I think my grandfather had a per-

fect worship for Byron and, if I may say so in all respect, that he sometimes carried it too far. Then I think that Byron had a great regard for my grandfather, but that occasionally he could not, to use a common phrase, refrain from pulling his leg. There was a real affection between them, out and out worship by my grandfather, and, on the part of Byron, entire faith and belief in him. There are many letters telling how my grandfather offered Byron all manner of assistance and others in which the poet would say, ' Don't tempt me ; you have already done too much.' "

It is pleasant to end our call at historic Albemarle Street on a personal note like that, so very characteristic of the Murrays in relation to their authors, great and small.

XIII

A LIBRARIAN'S ANECDOTAGE

WE often ask ourselves when we are young and have illusions, " Who would I like to be if I were not myself ? " It is a lovely question, because it lets us dally with things of the imagination at the time that the imagination is budding. It is a futile question, because if you were somebody else you would be quite different, and so you would just begin the inquiry all over again.

There is, however, another question which is more practicable : " What would I be if I were not what I am ? " It is more practicable, because, though we cannot change our personalities and identities, we can, and many people do, change our vocations.

Perhaps, as one grows older it is hardly worth while putting even that question, but in a healthy mind illusions are always trying to rout delusions. Myself, I often put it in a particular form, because when I look around and see business men so successful and so rich, I say, " Oh, to be a business man ! " Applying that to myself, I add, " What business man would I most like to be ? "

My considered answer is that I would like to be a librarian, because it is, if one may so describe it, business on one side and literary on the other. Thus I should not be taken away from my reading and writing, a robbery of these things being a disaster which is inconceivable.

Probably I first thought like this years and years ago, when I knew Mr. William Faux, who then presided over the circulating library of Messrs. W. H. Smith and Son, a house eminent in the business of newspapers and books. It is natural to be thinking of him, for he was one of the most true-born and gifted librarians that ever championed the fortunes of literature. He served, if I remember rightly, fully half a century under the flag of Smith, which to him was an emblem as dear as the heart of the Douglas was to his warrior followers. Necessarily in that time " Old Faux," as he was lovingly called, had many adventures with books and authors, and he told me some of them ; and now I am going to recall them for your benefit, more or less in his own words.

A LIBRARIAN'S ANECDOTAGE

A little incident, of which he was pardonably proud, had to do with the first story published by Thomas Hardy. Our Smith's librarian and William Tinsley, the publisher, met one day at the old Gaiety bar, a famous meeting place when London was Victorian. A manuscript was sticking out of Tinsley's pocket, and Mr. Faux asked who had written it. Tinsley answered that he thought it was by a new comer, but he had not had time to read it.

"Give it to me," said Mr. Faux, "and I will take it home and read it for you." He was attracted by the story, thought it clearly bespoke a great writer, and sent Tinsley the advice that he ought to publish it quickly. The novel fell flat until one of the weeklies gave it a belated review, when it jumped into circulation, and that was how, in 1871, 'Desperate Remedies' began its career and also began Thomas Hardy as an English novelist.

Another time, a member of the house of Macmillan, calling on Mr. Faux, said a word in direct recommendation of 'John Inglesant,' which was just coming out. Always anxious to hear of a good story, especially one well written and full of thought, Mr. Faux said he would read it and see what he thought of it. He did so, found it, in his judgment, to be a fine novel, and did everything he could to make it the success which it became. Perhaps one may add that the career of this study of the " Oxford movement " was greatly helped by the interest which Gladstone showed in it.

When Mr. Faux chatted about his library work, he was always careful to say that he did not do so in any spirit of vanity, but as showing what gleams of colour, what grateful little incidents might come into a circulating library. He was an early admirer of Stevenson, and recollected having bought cheap remainders of ' In the Cevennes,' and of ' An Inland Voyage.' They kept very well until Stevenson's triumph arrived, when they became worth more than their published prices ; and if one could get them to-day, they would be worth a lot more than their original prices.

One finds that bookmen, though they are not always inclined to adventure stories, all love Stevenson's ' Treasure Island,' probably because it is so very well written, so artistic in its composition, so finished in every detail. Mr. Faux liked it when he read it, before it was published in book form, and he ordered it largely for his library. Accordingly he had something of a sense of personal pride, when it won fame for Robert Louis Stevenson.

Again and again I would ask Mr. Faux, " What is it that causes a book to be read ; what gives it a start ? " and every time he answered very much in the same terms. He insisted that a book, whether a novel, or some other kind of work, must be worthy before it could achieve any lasting success. No book that had not quality, originality, personality, something to distinguish it and mark it out from the run of books, could do greatly. An author might log-roll it, a publisher might advertise it, anything might be done with it, but the public was not to be tempted unless there was a human savour in what was offered.

After that we came to another matter, namely : Given originality, talent, or even, if you like, genius, in a book, what was the subtle agency that brought it and readers together in the sympathetic way which means success for it and pleasure for them ?

Mr. Faux held, although he admitted the difficulty of answering such a question, that the greatest invitation to the reading of a new book was dinner-table talk. No doubt such talk was largely based on what people saw in the newspapers about new books, but the telling element was the personal recommendation.

Somebody read a newspaper review and learned that here was a particular book worth getting. Most likely, however, that somebody did not get it until a friend was met at the dinner-table who said : " I have just finished that book, and it is splendid. Order it at once from the library." Advice like that was acted upon, because it came directly, because it was individual.

There was a day when John Murray III. said to Mr. Faux that if a Murray book got a good review in ' The Times,' he was sure of selling the edition. Probably no single review anywhere would have an effect like that nowadays, when readers are so much more numerous, so much more democratic, and so much more scattered in their newspaper reading. Mr. Faux was sure, however, that when he heard a book the subject of keen dinner-table conversation, it was going to be largely read. " I have been reading such and such a book," somebody would begin. " What sort of book is it ? " somebody else would ask, and so its popularity would roll along, gathering speed as it rolled.

It was a pity Mr. Faux did not write his reminiscences as a librarian, because he had some amusing experiences which he could have told, apart from such general anecdotage as I have been recalling. As library subscribers do not write letters, unless they have a complaint to make, he was not, like a poor newspaper editor, deluged with correspondence. He once, however, got a letter from the writer of a book, saying he would like Smith's people to circulate it, but that, apparently, it was not on their list. This author was told that a record had been made of the book and that it would be got by the library if anybody wanted it. To this came the offer, would Smith's accept a copy, and a copy was duly accepted.

Well, some months later our obliging and pleasant author wrote saying he had been in six different parts of the country, and that at each place he had always been able to get his book from Smith's. He was entirely happy with himself and with Smith's. Dear fellow ! He had to be informed, in acceptable language, that the volume he had got every time was the very one which he himself had presented, and that it had only been out on those six occasions !

There was a touch of pathos in this little story, nor is it wanting in another which Mr. Faux had in his treasury. An author joined the library, paying twelve shillings, so as to be able to order a book written by himself, which it cost eighteen shillings to buy. Nobody else wanted it, but that did not upset the " Censor of the Strand," as Mr. Faux was sometimes called, quite unnecessarily, because he was the most broad-minded and gentle man in the world. He merely said that Smith's lost six shillings on their deal with that particular author, but that the human nature in it was worth the " banging " of the twelve sixpences.

If we knew everything, we should probably know that authors do occasionally write to the circulating libraries saying they have difficulty in getting particular books, without mentioning that these are books by themselves. Mr. Faux had many little epistles like that, and he could reply to them nicely, much preferring them to the more roundabout action of other authors, who remained silent themselves, so he said, but stirred up their friends to ask early and often for their new books.

Nobody knew more about the old-fashioned English three-volume novel than our friend, for he saw it reach its heyday of prosperity and he assisted it to an end. He thought it often permitted a writer, who otherwise would not have a chance, to make a beginning in authorship, because there was not much risk in publishing it at the price of a guinea and a half. He combated the idea, however, that the " three-volumer " was in any way an integral part of the circulating library, that the one could not exist without the other. It might, in some measure, have been a library invention, but he fancied that it belonged to the end of the eighteenth century when Walter Scott was becoming famous.

Speaking of the appearance of some three-volume novels which had made their mark, he recalled Benjamin Disraeli's ' Lothair.' That was his first great book as a politician, or, if one likes to turn the phrase about, his first book as a great politician. It was wonderfully read, far more widely read than Disraeli's ' Endymion,' which at first made infinite stir and then declined rapidly. When the librarians afterwards sold out their copies of this novel, for which, at trade price, they had paid more than twenty-one shillings, they only got half-a-crown for them. Well, one wonders if anybody would give even that to-day for any three-volume novel, if only because it takes so much space in a private library.

When William Faux reigned over Smith's library, English women had become by far the greatest readers of English novels, and he attri-

buted many of the " booms " to them. To-day
women are a still greater majority of our novel
readers, and it may even be that a larger percent-
age of all the books read are novels, though that
is hard to conceive. Once, by taking a little
census of the books which went out on circulation
from Smith's, Mr. Faux was able to establish that
eighty per cent. were fiction. He fancied that
this might be something like an average figure for
libraries throughout England, certainly in the
south of England. But he would point out that
as one goes farther north in these islands, people
read more serious literature. He did not know
why this should be, but perhaps he was right in
suggesting that the more vital climate of the north
stimulates a mind to more serious exercise.

What was the best advice that Mr. Faux could
give to an author wishful to write good books,
but, at the same time, books which would sell and
so enable him to keep writing ? His answer,
after he had thought over the question for a little
in his grave way, was this : " Give the very best
in yourself to your book, and then put it into
the hands of a publisher who will handle it well,
and especially advertise it well."

He added that there must be imagination in a
writer if he was to lay hold of his reader, who

otherwise would turn from a book calling it dry. So the supreme thing in a book is that it shall have the vague something which is personality, for, whether you call it talent or genius, it is the gift of the Literary Gods.

XIV

EPISTLES OF MARRIED LOVE

A REAL love story, told in letters written by the lovers, is the rarest thing in the world, and yet there are many real love stories. One does not mean passages between young people, so much as the sweethearting that goes on through a married life. Perhaps most married lovers do not write letters, anyhow, do not keep or publish them, and that is sensible, for, on paper, sentiment may easily become sentimentality. Not, however, in the case of Lord and Lady Wolseley, famous soldier and gifted lady, whose ' Letters,' edited by their old friend, Sir George Arthur, have been made public through the house of Heinemann.

Somebody, directed to the book by this writing about it, may say, " Ah, but these are not love-letters in the full sense of the term." Listen ! If a man and woman, husband and wife for more than half a century, write to each other in the tenderest, most intimate way, every day they are parted, what can such epistles be but love-letters ? Nay, they are true love-letters, as compared with some of those enshrined in literature, say, for example, George Sand's, which are letters of passion. Surely it is a finer thing to live sweetly in a love which is peace, than to dally in a passion which is war to the nerves. Anyhow, it is more comfortable, and—may one add, with a national apology ?—more English.

" There's nothing half so sweet in life as love's young dream ! " You may, dear man or lady, change your mind, or, at all events, allow for other possibilities, when you find Lord Wolseley saying to his wife, " I wonder, as I pray for you every morning and every evening, if you are, at the same time, praying for me " ; and she, writing to him, " I am more than a mother to you." Which of us would not desire a good woman to say that to us, knowing that it means the giving of her whole self, this divinity of motherhood being the ultimate treasury of all womanhood ? " My dearest husband," Lady Wolseley opens some letter, adding, within brackets, " Not that I have several " ; so you see she had that playful humour which, shining from a loyal heart, will hold a man graciously until he and his Joan have burnt all their fires and silently stolen away.

Never a puff of cloud darkened the atmosphere in which the Wolseleys lived, together, for each other, and for high purposes of service, because both were idealists, though he would call himself a man of action. " I would," he says in one of his letters, " infinitely prefer to lead some forlorn hope than to have written a Macaulay history, or any poem that Browning ever penned." When he met and talked with William T. Stead he wrote, " He is a sort of man who, in days of active revolution, might be a serious danger. I looked at him, thinking if it should ever be my lot to have to hang or shoot him." Not much of the idealist there, you make the comment, and yet that flavour runs through his letters, evoked, may be, by his wife. Still she was realist enough to say of Queen Victoria, hurrying along a corridor at Windsor, " She runs as if on castors," a living picture for Mr. Lytton Strachey.

But Queen Victoria never ran away from anything, least of all from the prerogative, which she had seized from the years, to rate her courtiers and even her advisers in national affairs. She said to Lady Wolseley, when there was trouble in the Soudan in the 'eighties, " I have been obliged to be very rude to them all, they are all so dilatory and tiresome." She also said, at the same time, that, though she needed rest, she dreaded to go abroad, " For I never know what they will do when my back is turned." Poor, dear, Royal lady, what would she have thought if she had still reigned in our day of clattering democracy ? But she liked Arthur Balfour, of whose youthful port Lord Wolseley writes, " I can't imagine how a man can exist with so little space allotted for boiler and internal mechanism." Naturally there has been a growth of territory in the Earl of Balfour.

There was so fine, so confident a love between the Wolseleys that, leaping the last ditch which may divide a husband and a wife, they could say brave, clever things to each other, or quote them from others. Addressing himself from Hatfield House on a Monday, the day after Sunday, his lordship observes to her ladyship that " The Prince de Joinville had some passages with Rachel," and that their correspondence began with a letter from him which consisted of " Quand, où, combien ? " No less brief was her answer, for her wit was no less : " Ce soir, chez moi, rien ! " " Go, my son," quoth a great Swedish Minister, " and see by what fools the world is governed," and Lord Wolseley recalled that for the " military folly," as he thought, which high-placed civilians sometimes talked to him. Could country-house life, as it often was in Victorian days, anyhow, be better described than in the French phrase " entre deux repas " ? Some country visit brought my Lord Wolseley into a moment's talk with the Lady Cardigan of a notorious volume of memoirs, and, says he to his wife, " The painted relic of past scandals lives in a most charming house."

The pen of Lord Wolseley could be quite caustic as well as graphic, and we find this when he goes abroad and writes of the people he meets. " She is," he says of the Empress of Kaiser William I of Germany, " certainly the most for-bidding-looking mortal I have ever laid eyes on —she is old, with a skin something of the colour of mustard. She is scraggy and was very *décol-letée*, with her face covered with powder, and a pair of painted eyebrows ! " But " hideous though she be, she certainly has the ability to make herself very agreeable and to say the right thing," for she showered compliments on Lord Wolseley. One gathers that he was always human enough and courtier enough not to be above the agreeableness of praise. Otherwise he would scarcely have had the nice diplomacy which helped to make him the " Only General " of his day.

Oh, there is no want of diversion, even, as will have been gathered, of piquancy, in the letters of the Wolseleys. But it is the married love of them which always holds, and how could it be otherwise when one reads the last letter signed " Garnet " ? " My dearest of dear women," it opens, and it goes on, " I love you as of yore, and I feel sure the last earthly thought that will pass through my brain, whilst dying, will be of you and for you. I pray that God will admit me into heaven, and when I get there, if I am permitted to do so, I shall take up a commanding position, past which all spirits and souls coming from our country must pass, so that I may be sure of meeting you." One can only say " Amen " in salute to a spiritual love like that of the Wolseleys, and it is well we should have it to know, though it was their own personal treasure.

XV

AN ESSAYIST OF LIFE

WHY is it that people who can write good
books are slow to do it, while those who
cannot are as fruitful as you like ? Sometimes
it may just be the chance of circumstances, but
there is a deeper, a more persistent, a less con-
querable reason, which belongs, as all things
belong, to human nature. A good book, that
is, a real book, has to have a mind, a heart and a
soul, and it can only get them from the writer.
This means such a giving out of personality that
emotional torture goes before, and physical
exhaustion comes after, and there is a natural
shrinking from both.

The baby of authorship is like the baby of
life, it testifies the labour of creation. It is the
divine visiting the earth, as nearly as it may, but
the beautiful joy has to be paid for, and the price
can be high. Does any of us know a friend,
gifted and crucified like this, who would not

rather run away for ever than sit down to a day's writing ? His case, or hers, is far worse, because the adventure ahead is known, than that of the bridegroom or the bride fearful of eloping alone when the marriage day actually comes. How enviable the other writing person who can crack it out without even sitting down to ink, but how unenviable the reader who falls that way !

One dreams in this manner over a little book, 'As You See It,' by " V.," which Sir Algernon Methuen set afloat. Memories rise of sensitive, poignant essays met somewhere in newspaper print and marked for a future life and salutation. Now that salutation to " V." of the ' Observer,' is also to Mrs. J. L. Garvin, the wife of its well-known editor, for here is a title-page with the secret. It is her maiden book, and yet there have been generations of literary blood on both sides of her family ; Sir Henry Taylor, of ' Philip van Artevelde' fame, Aubrey de Vere, Una Taylor, of the ' Edinburgh Review,' and the cultured Spring Rices. If she has not readily made herself accountable to that legacy of pedigree, the reason must be that she is so worthy of it, such a credit to it.

No pages in our English literature give it more glory than those written by its essayists, a Charles

Lamb of old, or an Augustine Birrell of to-day.
Since the Great War the English essay has had
a brave new blooming, and the battle caught the
pen of " V," " Where France's shoulder, if it
so might be, Naked and snowy, woos the Channel
Sea." You gather that she has poetry as well
as prose, and what you cannot fail to gather is
that she is an essayist distinctive by herself. She
makes a page of paper a page of life, or death,
as may be, not just an excursion in phrases, or a
travail in words, like the squirearchy of essayists
in this day. Her essays are herself, and if heavily
wise people, who write at each other, forgetting
the world, by the world forgotten, were to call
them impressions, why, it is no matter, because,
under that name, her roses, fragrant in their
natural wildness, smell quite as sweet.

Perhaps it is true to declare of Fleet Street,
that it has more trouble in " harpooning," " V.'s "
word about a policeman, a perfect paragraphist
than in finding a managing editor. Is it not
Mr. Kipling who says that the elimination of
the unessential is the true art of life ? We see
this, anyhow, in the difficulty of the paragraph,
the short story and the essay. " V." has the
gift of seeing instantly and clearly what matters,
and of leaving alone the rest. Similarly, she can

render what she sees into driving word pictures of the daily round, as we all know it. She is an idealist, without too many illusions or delusions, and, indeed, there is a verse in her book which might, for thought, philosophy and expression, be its spiritual motto :

" To live with justice, vision, and no hate :
  See without looking : see—but not without
  Giving slow judgment clemency's last doubt,
  Knowing too well the tyranny of fate—
  To live with justice, vision, and no hate."

The seeing eye and the revealing style ! Surely these are the true tools for the new English essay which is to outmatch even the old English essay, because it will tackle life straight and stark, and not merely life through the mirror of literature, through what others have written. " V." is at once a blazer and a master of this new model, and, in all, holding, diverting, an artist and a woman. We go with her to France, say, at Boulogne, to the cemetery, and " little chapels where the people were asleep," or, we go in search of a nun-nurse who, when found, looked old, but said she was thirty-two. She meant thirty-two " in the Lord," the time she had spent in the convent. " Why cannot we all be thirty-two in the Lord ? . . . the crudities, the agonies of spring are over, decay has not set in. It is an admirable age."

Most of us love to read thoughts which we would wish to be our own, and we love scarcely less a chorus of words that happily etches a sentiment. Somewhere in France " V." saw a " man who might have been a king," and " He put his long, close fingers over his drink with a gesture, loving, possessive, fearful, as if some one might take it away ; a gesture for a woman. . . . ! " Another man, also seen in France, was always writing a book, for his sins, no doubt. " Though he drank wine extravagantly, he wasted it in the glass, and now that I come to remember his face, it seems as if God had never quite finished that." There you feel the epigram in life before you have grasped its wording, and it might well leap from a French mentality. Leap the English Channel, however, and behold an English girl on the steps of a Belgrave Square house, waiting for her escort to the Ritz. " She has cool, bare arms, like arum lilies, ringless fingers, like tuberoses. How many generations of idleness, how much fine ignorance, has it taken to turn out this masterpiece ? "

If you are curious in a frankly human sense, if you want knowledge from the deeps of the

well and not from the nozzle of a fountain, then
you must ask, as it were, about the small things,
because mention of them does not scare, like
the pontifical things. " V." knows this ever so
instinctively, so she says, " Why is it that rouge
gives a woman as much confidence as a devout
lover ? " She answers, " It steadies her tired
nerves, it rallies her wit," and we must remember
that, even when there are only nerves, not wit.
Another problem put to us is, " What inherited
'phobia is it that makes people shrink from the
centres of restaurants ? " " V." makes no guess
at that, perhaps because it is so easy, or was
when nice people weren't supposed to go to
restaurants, even alone ! " It was one long,
unbroken procession of express letters, last inter-
views and first avowals " in Molly's sweethearting, and they nearly landed her a sad old maid.

Happily, " There comes a wind for every
sailor who is cunning with his sail." Even it
may have come to Chris, "A regular ballroom
girl, all white arms, wreaths and energy." She
may have known that " humour has many sources,
the brain, the heart," but one hopes she did not
know that too often its source is a " well of
bitterness." When we come up against that sort
of humour we learn how supreme may be the

bitterness of " Dropping Out." On that text
" V." has an essay so poignant that it positively
hurts, especially the woman who had always swept
a crossing in Belgravia until one Sunday morning
when she " fell down on the pavement in a ragged
heap." Yes, " It is only when the letter of one's
heart is threatened with missing the post, that
one notices the letter-box." Yes, also, " Life
has taught us to pass on, that the drunkard on
his feet too often steers again for the tavern " ;
but " It is he who sees the thing through to the
weary and solitary end, who is really distinguished
and worth while."

Mother Nature is a coarse savage when it
comes to the " dropping out," but you can hear
her saying with a croak and a chuckle, " At least
I give them lots of ways of going." There is
" The thin, tired woman," of a *casi di cura*, far
away, " who did her hair on top and only ate
macaroni. And of two tragedies, this last seemed
much the greater." Undoubtedly it would have
seemed so to Mrs. Morris, of Chelsea, " a patient
figure in a thin apron," and clearly, by that token,
a keeper of lodgings. But Mrs. Morris only
looked out of the window, searching the dark
heavens, when it was demanded of her, " Tell
me just once what makes the whole bally thing

worth while. Is it worth while ? Do you know ? Does anybody know ? Does nobody know ? " But Mrs. Morris understood Chelsea, and, taking her bearings from that anchorage, she found a philosophy all right. " Up West," quoth she, " the women have lovers because they can't afford to live without them. Down here the women don't have lovers because they can't afford to live with them—see ? "

Essays, indeed, of town and country life ! On the one hand we hear Mrs. Morris' " You're a good sort, you won't let one down. Only for some people life, like Jesus of Nazareth, passes by." On the other hand we visit a " sleeping water," a canal in the " deep green heart of the country," rich, not with the industry of labour, but with " the laziness of untroubled weeds." Should you linger by this sleeping water, notice how " The heron's flight is that of a celestial messenger bringing important, if not happy, tidings to an expectant people." A sonnet on the heron could not say more, unless Mrs. Garvin were to write it herself, for she must remember her literary call of the blood.

XVI

WERE THE VICTORIANS DULL?

DID you happen to hear a smart little story which was told about Mr. Lytton Strachey and his now famous study of ' Queen Victoria '? It was that he said : " I'll take a flat opposite the Albert Memorial, in Kensington Gardens, in order to write it."

Most likely he never threatened anything of the sort, because our younger authors never think, or do, half the bold, original things attributed to them. The moral here, however, was that, looking out on the Albert Memorial, he would be in constant touch with all that Victorianism was supposed to represent, a general dowdiness, if I may thus summarize the charge.

Queen Victoria reigned so long that she almost became a pillar of the Constitution, nay, a pillar of the world. She came, as it were, to stand for a great period of settledness, of quiet, gradual progress, no doubt, but also of convention. A smooth stream always runs deep, and in half a century it may make a wholly new course, though, day by day, week by week, month by month, and even year by year, this would hardly be apparent to the eye.

We know now that the England of Queen Victoria's coming to the throne, and the England of her death, were so different that the one would scarcely recognize the other. But yet, when the twentieth century cracked along, laden with all kinds of new ideas, plans and achievements, people fell into the habit of turning up their noses at the Victorians. "Yes," it was said loftily, " it was an age of crinolines and anti-macassars, of snug commercialism and *laissez-faire*."

When a young man, sure of himself and his time, steps into the shoes of an old man who, perhaps, has ceased to be sure of himself or his time, there is apt to be this cleverness, this belittling of what has been. By-and-by there is a reaction, for always any strain brings a rebound, and it soon began to show itself about Victorianism.

Was it so " cribb'd, cabin'd and confin'd" as some people thought it ? Was an age which lost the stage-coach, hooped petticoats and tight trousers, and gained railway trains, fast steam-ships and the electric telegraph, really so dull and commonplace as youth in the twentieth century regarded it ? Was a half-century which knew great novelists like Dickens and Thackeray, poets like Tennyson and Browning, statesmen like " Dizzy " and Gladstone, a dozen lawyers, journalists, artists and actors eminent beyond doubt, a half-century to be dismissed with a shrug and the remark, " We do better and we know better to-day " ?

Such a reflection upon the Victorian age has already, in most folk, given place to a true estimate of its greatness for England, for the world, and, when everything is said, for the well-being of mankind. We see definitely what some of the Victorians were prophets enough to claim in advance, that theirs was a time linkable for its riches with that of the Elizabethans. A constant outcoming of Victorian memoirs, headed by the letters of Queen Victoria herself, has been a strong force in making Young England of the twentieth century, realize what Old England of the nineteenth century really was. Those memoirs have been rich, sometimes also rare, and it is to the credit of our rising generation that it has been willing to read them with an open, receptive mind.

WERE THE VICTORIANS DULL?

Yes, Victorian England was great in material advances, still greater, perhaps, in some of the arts, certainly in literature. All this is definitely conceded as, willingly or unwillingly, it had to be, but one curious and serious doubt remains. Were people in the Victorian age happy? Weren't their lives restricted and narrow? Didn't they, in a word, live in days which, for all the light there was in them, might have been nights?

Here I am thinking of the inquiries suggested by Victorian memoirs, to close and critical readers. It is not, please note, an affair of the masses of the people, but of the upper classes and the cultured classes. They produce the memoirs, and they are to be judged by them, while evidence as to the well-being of the masses comes from other sources. How the masses have risen, in everything desirable, since Victoria ascended the throne, we all know, and it is a universal rejoicing. Also the upper classes have broadened in many manners and tolerances, there resembling democracy. But need this prove that in Victoria's day they lacked the satisfactions and joys of life?

With this, let us make a direct appeal to some of the recent Victorian memoirs, in order that their testimony may be consulted and sampled.

Quite a group of likely books leaps to the mind :
the late Canon Ainger's ' Memories of Eton,'
the ' Letters from England ' of an American,
Mrs. Bancroft, Miss Betham-Edwards's ' Mid-
Victorian Memories,' and Lord Ronald Gore's
' Old Diaries.'

Again, one thinks of Mr. R. C. Lehmann's
' Memories of Half a Century,' of Mr. Locker-
Lampson's ' My Confidences,' of Lady Frances
Shelley's ' Diary,' of Professor Knight's ' Retro-
spects,' of Mrs. Earle's ' Memoirs and Memories,'
or of Sir Edward Clarke's ' Story of my Life.'
The library of Victorian memoirs, issued within
easy memory, is quite large, for it also includes
Sir Algernon West's ' Recollections,' Madame
Waddington's ' Letters of a Diplomat's Wife,'
and, if you are interested in Parliamentary
affairs, Sir Henry Lucy's long ' Diary of a
Journalist.'

There is an endless stream of Victorian memories and memoirs, diaries and journals, at which
we Georgians, like the Edwardians of a decade
back, can refresh ourselves. Yes, and vastly
instruct ourselves. It is not possible to read
them all, and, bearing this in mind, I have made
a special choice of three of the newest and best,
all recently from the house of Murray, which has

stood very specially for English memoirs, such as we are studying. They are :

'Fifty-one Years of Victorian Life,' by the Dowager Countess of Jersey : 'A Romance of the Nineteenth Century,' by Colonel Dudley Ward, and 'Lady Rose Weigall,' by her daughter, Miss Rachel Weigall.

What we have to consult them about is very simple : the kind of life which was Victorian, early, middle, or later, and whether, when we get down to the confidences of those who lived and knew, it was in the least dull or contracted, or what a Georgian maiden of this whistling twentieth century would call " stupid." Georgian maidens are not " stupid," and indeed they see so clearly with their bright eyes that they find it hard to sympathize with the sight of their grandmothers. Nay, they even seem to have senses and feelings of which their grandmothers knew nothing and that makes them a trifle uncanny.

" People," writes Lady Jersey, " are apt to talk and write as if Early Victorian and Mid-Victorian children were kept under strict control and made to treat their elders with respectful awe. I cannot recall any undue restraint in our case. . . . Our mother was an influence which no one would have attempted to resist, but she never interfered with any reasonable happiness or amusement. Our father was the most cheerful of companions, loving to take us about to any kind of sights or entertainments which offered, and buying us toys and presents on every possible occasion."

You see there a mother and a father very much as they would be to-day, and as fathers and mothers always have been and will be, loving and seeking the happiness of their little folk. "The only constraint put upon us," adds Lady Jersey, "which is not often used with the modern child, concerned religious observance. We had to come in to daily prayers at ten o'clock, even if it interfered with working in our gardens or other out-door amusement, and church twice on Sundays was the invariable rule. . . ." She was made to learn any number of chapters and hymns and Scripture catechisms, not to speak of the Thirty-nine Articles. When her mother and governess failed to find enough of these sweet exercises for her, they turned her on to Thomas à Kempis, and she survived.

It is clear, therefore, that the Victorian child was well grounded in religion, as to which Lady Jersey says, "On the whole, I feel sure that the advantage of acquiring so many great truths, generally in beautiful language, far outweighed any passing irritation that a young girl may have felt with these religious obligations."

We know what dancing is like to-day, or, perhaps, we don't know, and still, as the soldiers used to say, " carry on." Naturally, anyhow, we are interested in hearing from Lady Jersey that, in her early days, there was still a " sort of question as to the propriety of waltzing." She tells us that valses and square-dances were danced alternately at balls, and a few, but very few, girls were limited to the latter. Chaperones, who have now, in effect, disappeared like the Dodo, were almost a law of the Early Victorian social world, certainly a rule of correctness. Girls went back to them between dances, and it was not until later that " sitting-out " became a custom.

We shall test the Victorian age in another way, in Colonel Dudley Ward's ' Romance of the Nineteenth Century,' for it is largely a book of love letters. How did nice, well-bred, gently-born folk make love about the time of Waterloo, which may be called the military salute to the coming of Victoria and all her reign stood for ?

There is a charming answer in many epistles

exchanged between the Rev. George Brett and Dorothy Best, before they became a devoted and happy man and wife. She was a better letter writer, and perhaps a better lover than he was, but always they got on quite well, allowing for the conventions of their time. George was rather slow to overcome them, but knowing that was all, she sets out " To tell you how truly I feel your tender professions of love to me and how much it will ever be my study to preserve your affection. . . . To make your happiness through life will be ever my first wish. Believe that to hear from you is my greatest comfort when absent."

No doubt cheap postage, the telegraph, and especially the telephone, have made away with the fine round-handness which belonged to Early Victorian love letters. What is that, however, but a loss to sweethearts, so why lampoon Victorianism ? " Was it," George Brett wrote, " possible to increase the affection I feel towards you, it would certainly be augmented by the very kind and handsome manner in which you immediately answered a message which, I am ashamed to say, I conveyed to you in a very slovenly way. I assure you your letter poured balm into the breast of the venerable old lady, my Mama, whose spirits previously were very low, through indisposition."

George was in much better form when, remembering the counsel of an " eminent Lord " about letters, he said : " Embellishments of style imply study and deep thought, which give a stiff and formal character to letters. One discomposure of the auburn tresses on your forehead, conveys more delight from the natural ease and freedom of sentiment, than a folio of studied phrases and deep-thought expressions."

We are more " advanced," more natural, anyhow, when we come to the second love correspondence in Colonel Dudley Ward's book, that of Baliol Brett, who became a Master of the Rolls and first Viscount Esher, and Eugénie Mayer, his wife. They met in the late 'forties of last century, and straightway he fell in love with her dark beauty and her brilliant mind. " Day and night," he addressed her, " I have no thought, however dull and ugly in itself, through which the thoughts of you, which never leave me, do not twine like roses through an arbor, and render it beautiful by the excess of their beauty."

He loved her in a thousand ways, for a thousand things, and " I long, with the most passionate eagerness, for the day when I may press you to my heart in full security that you are indeed my wife." Eugénie was colder, or, perhaps, only as became a woman, more reserved to begin with, but soon her heart warmed into a flame. She did not want money in a husband, but she did want to see him succeed in his profession, and when, gladly taking all risks, they married, she wrote, " Never fear for one instant that your little wife can love you less. Her life is so entirely yours that nothing can happen to give you one little cloud in what you call heaven. Love you I always will, and my only wish, when I leave your arms, will be to return to them, to repeat always, always, I love you."

One wonders whether, in our very up-to-date day, we have preserved the art of love letters with that richness and beauty. If not, the point is one in favour of the Victorians, who, when they liked, at least knew how to express themselves, and there is many a token of this in our third Victorian witness, the ' Memoirs of Lady Rose Weigall.' She was the last survivor of the intimate friends of the Duke of Wellington, and her life-story gives us many glimpses of him. He, no doubt, was regarded as the Great Victorian, though, indeed, his name and fame had

been won before the young daughter of the
Duchess of Kent trod the throne.

At the same time he is only one of many great
Victorians that find mention in the friendships
of Lady Rose Weigall, whose girlhood implied
serious studies and the memory of them. She
went in for good reading and for making copious
extracts·on books and their characters, seasoning
them with her own observations and comments.
This wisdom, gathered and original, she put into
yearly journals, to which she also confided the
ideas and thoughts suggested by her daily life.

Probably our Georgian girls do not keep diaries
in the same serious " high-brow " fashion, and that
may be a loss to them, to us, and to those who
will come later. If Lady Rose Weigall had been
neglectful we should not have had the entry :
" Nothing can be less prepossessing than Dickens'
appearance. His action is not graceful, his voice
is not musical and rather hoarse, and yet he
moves masses of people of all ages and of all
kinds alternately to tears and laughter, to a degree
I never saw equalled."

Nor should we have had a precious paragraph
about rugged, Scottish Thomas Carlyle and his
brilliant wife, Jane Welsh Carlyle. She said to
somebody, in her burring Scots accent, that " Car-

lyle, like all men, is a fidget about everything ; but when he sits of an evening smoking and begins a denunciation of everything, commencing with the universe and ending with a pair of shoes, I just sit still, and when he has done, I say, ' Yes, my dear, it's all verra true, and now we'd better go to bed.' "

Is there, half a century later, any better way of managing a husband laden with genius, like Thomas Carlyle, or any husband whatever ? And if that be so, does it not suggest that humanly, as well as generally, the Victorians, great and small, " knew their way about," as we would now say ? They were, in their blood and brains, minds and manners, joys and griefs, of the time which was their time. It influenced them and they moulded it, by large deeds and large personalities, and when next any of us thinks to belittle the Victorian Age, let all that be remembered.

XVII

THE DIARY IN ENGLISH LETTERS

DO you keep a diary ? You may or you may not. Anyhow you are interested in diaries, because they make good reading. Our English literature is particularly rich in them, and one wonders why that should be. One may always wonder.

It cannot be that English men and women are more egotistic—or egoistic, for there is a clear difference between those words—than the men and women of other nations. They think of us as a reserved people, and we are, in many ways, self-conscious, sometimes to the degree of silent awkwardness.

When you reflect, it may just be this English reserve which has driven us to the keeping of diaries. We have felt that we could, at all events, be confidential with them, however we might be with our friends, not to speak of strangers. Mostly, too, folk who keep diaries mean them never to be published, and those of us who are old enough can remember, in token of this, little volumes with locks on them which used to be sold for diary keeping. They seemed uncouth and harsh, and in a day of more candour and, perhaps, rather less self-consciousness, they have gone out of fashion.

If you want to know all about English diaries, and the curiosity is both human and literary, you should turn to a recent book 'English Diaries' by Mr. Arthur Ponsonby, M.P., Under Secretary for Foreign Affairs in the Labour Government. Within its pages you will find a review of English diaries from the sixteenth to the twentieth century, or from King Edward VI. as diarist to Queen Victoria, also as a diarist, and later.

"No kind of reading," writes Macaulay, "is so delightful, so fascinating as this minute history of a man's self." Our most recent capture has been the journal of Joseph Farington, the eighteenth century artist and man about town. He had no literary quality worth speaking about, but then literary quality is often the last thing one wants in a diary. It tends to "fine writing," and "fine writing" tends to phrases rather than to facts, and all that makes away from the sound, honest record ; something meeting the description by Robert Burns of facts as " chiels that winna' ding an' daurna' be disputed."

Any of us, the learned or the most illiterate, the known person or the quite unknown person, may keep a diary, which is not, if you please, history, unless in very exceptional cases, but the story of a human life amid its surroundings. Nor is a diary an autobiography in the actual meaning of that word, because the one may contain anything, and be ever so scrappy, while the other is more or less a continuous narrative, set down to be published. Again, letter writing has little relationship to diary-keeping, because there is always the consciousness that there is a reader waiting at the other end of the post. Thus the writer becomes self-conscious, and the " truth, the whole truth, and nothing but the truth," never flows from a pen so used.

" We may claim, therefore," in Mr. Arthur Ponsonby's admirable summing-up, " that diary writing is a unique form of writing. The literary, the learned, and the great, by no means necessarily excel in this particular art. It is confined to no one class, no one profession, no one age of life. Sovereigns, scholars, sportsmen, tradesmen, philosophers, old women and children, all write diaries."

Those of us who saw something of Gladstone, know that he kept a diary for many years, and that its contents proved of no great use when Viscount Morley came to write his biography. King Edward VII. kept a journal, so instructed, when he was young, by Queen Victoria and the Prince Consort. Queen Victoria's own diary must be the most extensive work of the sort that exists in the English language. It was begun when she was thirteen, and was kept up until the end of her life. She lived to be eighty-two, and the diary harvest of that long life makes a hundred volumes of manuscript.

This great journal, which is never likely to be all published, gets its distinction from the fact that it is the chronicle of a Sovereign. It will be a priceless document for historians of the Victorian age, because it will both reveal the inner forces at work making history, and test the accuracy of other sources of information. Queen Victoria had her limitations as a woman and no doubt also as a Sovereign, but she had, as the saying is, " no axes to grind." Her position was far too great, her personality far too strong, for the frailties of common humanity always to be coming in, as they do with some diarists, and so her journal may almost be regarded as a State paper.

THE DIARY IN ENGLISH LETTERS

Now when one has said that, one comes upon the essential difference which there is between the English diary and the French, the Italian, or the European diary generally. We make diaries out of the events that pass around us and the men and women we see, or meet, or know, and often they are very interesting diaries. Samuel Pepys is full of gossip concerning other people and the events of his time, though, happily for our entertainment, he never forgets himself. John Evelyn is even more a general recorder and so is Charles Greville, whose diaries, when they were published, quite upset Queen Victoria, because he held an official position as Clerk of the Council.

Think of the European diaries which have made a stir, for instance, that of George Sand, who was French, or that of Marie Bashkirtseff, who was Russian, and you say to yourself, " Yes, they were, in effect, self-revelations, self-stories, the intimate lives, spiritual and physical, of the people who wrote them." It was so, but always it should be borne in mind that the average diary of a foreigner is not likely to reach us in English ; only the one so explosive in its humanity that it becomes a confession for all mankind.

Not long ago, however, we got ' The Journal of a Disappointed Man,' and ' A Last Diary,' a

work which is almost un-English in its intimacy
and therefore to be grouped with a chronicle like
that of Marie Bashkirtseff. It shows, among
other things, that the tendency of modern life,
even among a people of reserve like ourselves,
is to become more introspective, more self-analy-
tical. Nay, it shows self-analysis carried into
very deep recesses of human consciousness, for
" Barbellion," as the writer called himself, had a
burden of qualities which made for that.

He was the son of a journalist and himself did
some journalism, although weak health must
have stood in the way when a strenuous profession
was concerned. He was born in Devonshire in
1889, and, from work on his father's paper, he
went to a post in the Natural History Museum at
South Kensington. He died in 1919, after living
long enough to see his first diary into print and
the second one completed in manuscript. He
cut no figure in the world, he met no celebrities,
he probably never even saw the King, there being
much unlike Mr. Arthur Ponsonby who was born
in the atmosphere of the court ; and yet he left a
diary which will, for its sheer human interest,
rank high in this corner of English literature.

How hard it is for the most willing, the most
conscientious diarist to tell the truth absolutely

about himself. " It is," writes " Barbellion," whose real name was Cummings, " impossible to tell the truth. In this journal I have tried, but I have not succeeded. I have set down a good deal but I cannot tell it. Truth of self has to be left by the psychology-miner at the bottom of his boring." Again, when the night of death was closing round him, he reflects, " In the Journal, I can see now that I have made myself out worse than I am, or was. I even took a morbid pleasure in intimating my depravity—self-mortification. . . . I don't think, on the whole, my portrait of myself does me justice."

There we have a diarist come to judgment, and it is a frequent position when a man or woman tries to write on paper what really can only be felt in the emotions, not written. " I am so steeped in myself," is another of " Barbellion's " confessions, " in my moods, vapours, idiosyncrasies, so self-sodden, that I am unable to stand clear of the data, to marshal and classify the multitude of facts and thence draw the deduction what manner of man I am. I should like to know, if only as a matter of curiosity. . . . A fool, of course, to start with—but the rest of the diagnosis ? "

One asks if diarists influence each other in

their outlook, in what they write, and in general ways. One so asks because we have, from " Barbellion," the deliverance, " My father was Sir Thomas Browne and my mother Marie Bashkirtseff. See what a curious hybrid I am ! She feels as I feel ; we have the same self-absorption, the same vanity and corroding ambition. She is impressionable, volatile, passionate, ill. So am I. Her journal is my journal." Clearly our introspective young Englishman had read the Bashkirtseff journal into his own life and that may, in some measure, account for the un-English touch, as I have ventured to call it, in his liferecord.

Eminently English, in style, manner and thought, are two diaries of distinction which the Great War has thrown to us amid its mass of literature. One of them, kept by Lord Bernard Gordon-Lennox, has only been published privately, if at all, but we have extracts from it by Mr. Arthur Ponsonby. The other, entitled, ' The Diary of a Dead Officer,' was written, as we learn, by Mr. Arthur Graeme West. He was a civilian soldier and officer in the Great War, that is to say, he had not been a regular soldier, before the war, like Lord Bernard Gordon-Lennox. The interest of considering their journals,

side by side, is that one writes with the dry blunt-
ness of a gallant " Diehard," and that the other
shows all the reaction of thought which Armageddon caused among our young men of mentality.

On August 12, 1914, Gordon-Lennox went
over from Southampton to Havre with the second
battalion of the Grenadier Guards, in which he
was a major. When the ship reached the French
port, it was received with cheering, and " We
responded by singing the Marseillaise, which
caused a continual ' 'eep 'eep 'ooray ' in return."
A plain, matter of fact entry, you see, and it is the
same with our soldier of the pre-war school when
he comes to speak of the retreat from Mons. " I
don't think any of us wishes to go through such a
trying time again. Also the British army is not
accustomed to retiring."

Hard war times they were, and they needed a
Spartan philosophy such as this plain diarist gave
them. " I had," he writes of a near escape, "just
taken off my coat and laid it on the back of the
trench, about a yard away, when there was a tremendous explosion above me. The man in the
pit, next door, was badly hit by a shell, my coat
had the right arm nearly taken off at the shoulder
and the left sleeve cut to bits, and it was only a

yard off me, but I am thankful to say I was not inside the coat at the time." There we have an acceptance, quietly, definitely, of what goes with war, perhaps of war itself, as an inevitable thing in an imperfect world.

We find a different catechism in ' The Diary of a Dead Officer,' and Lord Bernard Gordon-Lennox also made the great sacrifice. Arthur Graeme West wants to know, and then he wants to say what he knows, often by bitter experience. " One noted first their inability to teach us anything," he declares of his early military instructors, " because there were too many superannuated old martinets trying to do it at the same time ; secondly, the lack of doctrine among them all ; even if they could have taught, they knew nothing. The way we were taught musketry was laughable," and he laughs almost so that we can hear him.

By-and-by we have even a fine spirit like Arthur Graeme West " fed up," as the soldiers put it, with the war and its torture. " I am," he writes, " a creature caught in a net. Most men fight, if not happily, at any rate patiently, sure of the necessity and usefulness of their work. So did I —once ! Now it all looks to me so absurd and brutal that I can only force myself to continue in a kind of dream state. I hypnotize myself to undergo it."

A diary just like that would scarcely have been written by an English officer before the twentieth century. Its self-analysis and its war-analysis are characteristic of the English generation which is now to be in power. Most likely this generation will give a new form, a new turn, a new meaning to many things, as well as to the English Diary.

XVIII

SHORT STORIES OF QUALITY

DO you read short stories? Probably you do when you come across them in magazines, in weekly papers, and in daily papers, for they may now be found there. On the other hand, you probably turn away from a book of short stories.

Has it ever occurred to you to ask why this should be? There is really no reason for it except, perhaps, a little prejudice, which somehow is characteristic of English readers.

One fancies that the long reign of the three-volume novel had something to do with the inability of the short story, almost for an equally long time, to find any great place in English literature. A whole generation was nourished on the " three-volumer," as it was called in the days of later Victorian writers like Wilkie Collins, Anthony Trollope, William Clark Russell, and Blackmore, the author of ' Lorna Doone.'

SHORT STORIES OF QUALITY

How surprised those old novelists would be, even Charles Dickens and William Makepeace Thackeray, if they could look up and see the many books of short stories which appear to-day. Here is a list, compiled with some care, of perhaps the best present-time volumes of short stories. It is not implied that they will all appeal to all readers. Some will, some may not. Simply I give the list as one of short stories that have had a real, current success, in book form :

'Where the Pavement Ends' and 'In Dark Places,' by John Russell.

'Miss Bracegirdle and Others' and 'The Love-a-Duck and Other Stories,' by Stacy Aumonier.

'Short Shipments' and 'Old Wine in New Bottles,' by Elinor Mordaunt.

'The Four Million' and 'The Gentle Grafter,' by O. Henry.

'The Vrouw Grobelaar's Leading Cases' and 'The Second-Class Passenger,' by Perceval Gibbon.

'Tales of Mean Streets' and 'Green Ginger,' by Arthur Morrison.

'Captures,' by John Galsworthy.

'To Tell You the Truth,' by Leonard Merrick.

' The Empty House,' by Algernon Blackwood.

' The Pleasant Husband,' by Marjorie Bowen.

' Uncanny Tales,' by May Sinclair.

' Told at the Plume,' by Eden Phillpotts.

' Men, Maids and Mustardpot,' by Gilbert Frankau.

' These Charming People,' by Michael Arlen.

It is not enough to make lists of the best books of short stories ; and so one goes on to take this one as a text for where we English people are in regard to the short story. It does not stand so high with us as it does with the French, but you do not need to be told that, if you know anything about French literature. Maupassant was a great writer of the short story, or, as it is called in French, the *conte*, which means, if one may so express it, a short story done with literary quality.

Now, that is what our short stories have rather lacked in the past. The English world of fiction was so essentially the long novel, that men and women of writing talent gave little attention to anything else. They said to themselves, " Why should we trouble about a kind of art which does not seem to be native to English readers ? It would be very beautiful to master it, and to per-suade English readers to read it, but that is to undertake a pilgrimage. As it is, there is an endless demand for long novels, and when one has succeeded with one of them, one is almost compelled to go on in that manner."

You see, therefore, that the attitude of what one may call the old-fashioned English public towards the short story, also determined the attitude of the author towards it. It would be a curious person who deliberately set out to write something for which there was no likelihood of success, and it would be very discouraging. The consequence was that a quarter of a century ago, most of the English short stories written were really fragments of long stories rather than the complete, beautiful little things which we associate, not only with French authors like Maupassant, but with American writers like Edgar Allan Poe.

He was one of the greatest masters there has been of the short story which is distinct from the French *conte*, meaning a story of high drama as well as of literary distinction. It is scarcely too much to say that Edgar Allan Poe is the father of the American short story, and when that is said, it should be remembered that the American short story has, in recent years, greatly influenced the English short story.

Bret Harte, who lived a good deal in this country, and who died here, was also a master of the short story, as take, to mention one gem among his writings, ' The Luck of Roaring Camp.' He had done his best work when he came to England to settle, but there is no doubt that his presence among us did much to influence English writers interested in the craft and technique of the short story.

What helped it from the first in America was that magazines like the ' Century,' ' Scribner's,' and ' Harper's ' all wanted fine work of this kind, and were willing to pay well for it. Therefore an American writer found it easier to " place " short stories than long stories, a reversal, you perceive, of the English situation. But when the ' Century ' and ' Scribner's ' and ' Harper's ' had a large sale, as they once had, in this country, they drew upon English writers of ability. That circumstance gave a certain helpfulness to the eventual rise of the short story on our side of the Atlantic, for its position to-day is infinitely stronger than it was a quarter of a century ago.

Will you please appreciate, then, that the two literatures of the world which have done most for the short story are those of France and America. But there is no reason why we should not do as much for it as they have done, and, allowing for our fertility in authorship, even more. One may say that with some assurance, because, at last, we really have reached a point where people, even ordinary readers, do take an interest in the short story when it appears in book form, and that is something like a small revolution.

Not long ago it was nearly useless for a publisher's traveller to take an advance copy of a volume of short stories round the booksellers and hope to get a good "subscription." He simply could not do it, because the booksellers knew that their readers did not care for reading of this sort, and that, therefore, any examples of it would, most likely, remain on the shelf. No bookseller likes to order literature which is going to meet with that fate, because every bookseller, if he is to succeed, must be a business man as well as a man fond of books, if he always is that? He would tell you that the chief enemy, if one may put the thing rather strongly, of short stories was the English woman who always said she could not be bothered with them.

When one says that, one gets back to the influence which Victorian reading had upon Victorians, and it lasted until the younger people of our own generation began to think for themselves and read for themselves. It was difficult, perhaps, to make a good short story out of a purely domestic situation, because character and even, to a certain extent, human problems have to come into it, if it is to be a drama within a very limited space.

With the long novel you could wander about here and there and everywhere, and if the writer was interesting personally it did not much matter whether his plot was well knit or not, whether his characters were really human people, or whether they were merely stock figures. No short story, however, could be written in that way, because the essence of it is that every word must tell, that there must be no superfluous word in it, and that it must go along rapidly from its beginning to its end.

We have seen, within our own experience, how brilliantly English can be used for short-story writing. The high master of it in our time has been Mr. Rudyard Kipling, and no doubt his ' Plain Tales from the Hills ' did more to blaze a highway for it into our modern literature, than any other event that has happened. Some of his stories appeared in ' Macmillan's Magazine,' which, like ' Longman's Magazine,' ' Blackwood's Magazine,' and other magazines once issued from book-publishing houses, took trouble to get good short stories, because they had readers who liked such reading and could appreciate it.

There was the other reader, he of the popular magazine, who did not want too good stories, and to whom Kipling's 'Plain Tales' would have been over-fine, the reader who only wanted something stirring. Now that has led to a kind of short story for which a French master of the art would rebuke us, something that is interesting enough to read in an ordinary way, but not artistic. Every magazine meant for popular circulation, is filled with such stories, and they are quite good, very wholesome, and very well paid for. They are not, however, short stories of the calibre of Kipling, for his may ultimately rank even with those of Edgar Allan Poe.

What has happened all round is that the purely popular tale has gone up in art, while the artistic tale, without coming down in quality, has got its own public. When Katherine Mansfield died everybody said, "We have lost a writer of exquisite short stories," and so we did. We have still, fortunately, other writers not less good, and one thinks of Sir Arthur Conan Doyle and his 'Sherlock Holmes,' or, again, of Mr. Perceval Gibbon and of Mr. Stacy Aumonier, whose extraordinary lightness of touch gives readability to everything he writes.

There are still many English authors of fiction

who content themselves with long novels, only now and then producing a volume of short stories which are just chips from their workshops. But, fortunately, we are creating a real school of short-story writers, men and women who place that difficult art—because the short story is extremely difficult to do—before the writing of novels.

The change has come, for one reason, because there is to-day a much better short-story market in England. That is the practical side of things, and, indeed, any editor of almost any magazine will tell you that he has real difficulty in getting enough good short stories. It is perfectly true, and so anybody who thinks of authorship might very well think of the short story, because it is a road which will lead to good fortune if the necessary literary abilities are present. It is much better for a young writer to be appearing with short stories in the magazines, than to be toiling away for years at a long novel which may never have a public at all. The short story is the paragraph of fiction, because it has to be shapely and complete in itself, not merely what we have called a fragment of a longer tale. Mr. Gilbert Frankau, an admirable writer of short stories, always begins his long novels from the end and works backwards, as it were. He certainly could

not do that with a short story, because it is necessary before you start writing, to know what
will happen all through. There is the beginning,
the setting of the plot ; there is the middle, the
working of it out ; and there is the climax when
the whole fruit of what has been written comes to
a head.

It will be asked, perhaps, if an English writer
is likely, with short stories, ever to win the fame
that Scott, Dickens, or Thackeray won with
novels ? Nobody can answer that, but it is certain
that Mr. Rudyard Kipling's short stories will
keep his fame green when, perhaps, some of his
long ones have been forgotten. Everybody
cannot hope to be a Kipling, since that means
genius, but at least he has shown what a wonderful literary field there is to-day for the right
kind of recruit.

Mr. John Galsworthy, a graver writer, has
proved the same thing, and if, after what has
been said, you still have the idea that short stories
do not interest you, will you please get his ' Captures,' and see if they are not compelling reading.
We owe a good deal to Mr. Galsworthy, as well
as to Mr. Kipling, to Mr. W. W. Jacobs, to Mr.
Leonard Merrick and to others, but the fact upon
which we may entirely congratulate ourselves is

that at last the short story in English literature is comparable, artistically, to the short story of America or France, and to say that is to give it very great praise.

XIX

MUDIE'S IN HISTORY

MUDIE'S has been the mirror of fashion in English literature for more than three-quarters of a century. It is not simply a name for a great circulating library, but a national institution. Mudie's is a tradition for the general stream of English reading in its time, and so also for English authorship, because the two live on each other. Therefore it is not too much to say that here has been a clearing-house for English thought, habits, and deeds, as these have swung into the eternal Sea of Print.

Certainly, if you want to know the real English reader, man or woman, in particular the reader of London Society and the London middle classes, you must go and ask Mudie. " He, being dead, yet speaketh " ; for the spirit of Charles Edward Mudie, who invented the modern circulating library, still lives in New Oxford Street, across from the British Museum. Personality was in

163

it all, as it is in everything original or lasting, and the Mudie Touch has not lost itself to-day, as we shall see.

Do you happen, yourself, to be in a public line of business ? If so you will, now and then, get queer, weird letters from people. You keep those letters, because they are a hall-mark of confidence in you. Mudie's archives contain epistles like that, one of them saying, " Please be so good as to reply to my letter respecting the book entitled ' Harry Stottell's Works.' " You need a moment to discover that the request was for ' Aristotle's Works ! ' " Send me," another subscriber wrote, ' Bath Under Bone Ash,' " instead of ' Bath Under Beau Nash ' ! Particularly wanted was ' The Uncomical Traveller,' by Charles Dickens, but the applicant only got ' The Un-commercial Traveller.' More difficult to meet was the demand, " If you haven't anything recent by Julius Cæsar, give me something about him."

It was the war which brought to Mudie's an order for ' Blackmore's Alsace-Lorraine.' Most likely a prompt copy of his novel, ' Alice Lor-raine,' caused disappointment. It took longer to puzzle out,' A Darn Bee,' by " Gelliott," as George Eliot's ' Adam Bede.' Of course, ' Green Car Nation ' meant that once stirful novel, ' The

Green Carnation.' 'Paternoster Row,' by George Gissing, was identified as implying his ' New Grub Street.'

Many well-known people have been constant readers and visitors at Mudie's ; some, what you might call " habitués." Gladstone, the last English super-statesman who pilgrimaged among the old bookshops in search of a " find," was frequently in the library. He was never in quest of new books, which, indeed, fell upon him at Hawarden like leaves, thanks to authors hopeful of an acknowledging post-card. What he sought was a likely bargain in some volume or edition that concerned his own subjects, say Bishop Butler or Horace.

If he knew Gardiner, the historian, and Samuel Butler, the author of ' Erewhon,' he might easily have run against them at Mudie's, for they were often there. So was Richard Garnett, of the British Museum, and certainly the G.O.M. knew and esteemed him as a Grand Old Bookman. Another frequent visitor was Cardinal Manning, a smiling pillar of asceticism, embodying the faith and traditions of the Middle Ages transmuted into the spirit of modern progress.

Oh ! Mudie's has caught the echo of many a famous foot, the Ionic columns in the large saloon have looked down on many a face with a name. One picturesque figure was David Christie Murray, the novelist, in his velveteen jacket, mostly the same jacket. More picturesque still was Whistler, the artist, who would look in and ask whether anybody was reading his 'Gentle Art of Making Enemies.' Not many people were, when it was new, but copies of the book are now worth stealing.

Darwin's 'Origin of Species' appeared in 1859, four years after Mudie had moved from Southampton Row, where he began most modestly in 1844. There had been 'The Voyage of the *Beagle*' in 1840, and there was to be 'The Descent of Man' in 1871. These books, with the corresponding writings of Thomas Henry Huxley, Alfred Russel Wallace, John Tyndall, and other master men, stood for perhaps the greatest single leap forward in knowledge that the world has known, and they took their message through the door of Mudie's and out again.

Science and religion ! Mudie's looked on at the conflict, was a good servant in it, although we, in more charted waters, can now see that there was no conflict but merely a new assessing of values. 'Draper's Conflict' was a target in the fray, and yet how often, in this present year of grace, has a battered copy of it had to be handed over Mudie's counter ? Hardly ever, one ventures to say.

Then the song of social reform came piping down New Oxford Street in William Morris's 'Dream of John Bull,' and 'News from Nowhere.' The note of spiritualism, meaning, broadly, belief in another life in another world, was sounded by F. W. Myers. It has been echoed still more definitely by Sir Oliver Lodge, Father Hugh Benson, Sir Arthur Conan Doyle, and a growing host of writers.

The ghosts of many a cause, won, lost, or still in doubt, walk the corridors of Mudie's. They knew the blast that Mrs. Lynn Linton blew out of the west for the woman's movement. Dear lady ! what a daring person she was supposed to be, and so dangerous ! She was earlier than Sarah Grand and 'The Heavenly Twins,' and may be she was not as " advanced." It was her friend, amiable Grant Allen, who carried the woman's red flag of revolt to the hill-top and there planted it.

Again Mudie has looked on the pageant of progressive ideas, taking his part in it, more or less, or refusing to take any part as he conceived right, from the standpoint of a " select library."

But always he was there, always he was going out into the world with his boxes of books.

Most folk think only of Mudie's in novels, which is quite wrong, and yet, in a sense, quite right. The great traffic has been in novels and so will be, for the simple reason that the story is the literary thing common to everybody, old and young, educated or not. The traffic in other writings, biography and autobiography, travel and history, *belles-lettres* and poetry, is also, however, very great. The ordeal of our long war-time made it greater, and yet the return of the average reader, the reader in mass, is ever to the novel. Why not ? Everything comes within it. Nothing, nowadays, is left out of it, assuredly not if Mr. H. G. Wells can help that.

Most men read novels for recreation, as Lord Russell of Killowen used to read a " shocker " after a hard day, and as Mr. Lloyd George does to-day. Therefore men send their office-boys to Mudie's for stories with stir and " go " in them, and sometimes, may be, for others, not always " in stock," which cry a different appeal. But " action " is the man's fodder in fiction, the blow and the blood, unless he be a " literary fellow," and then he seeks, often, anyhow, the " analytical novel."

Now, the woman, whether she be governed
alone by her sex-instinct or by that set in a fram-
ing of intelligence, education, intellect, is a better
novel-reader than a man. She begins, though
she may not know it, with a full understanding of
the title of Charles Lamb's essay, ' The Pleasures
of Anticipation.' That is what every woman
knows on the literary high-road, and naturally it
carries her over the hills and far away in the pages
of fiction.

She reads, if she be any real woman at all, for
a stimulus of thought and feeling, which, in her
case, may be more powerful, and, therefore, even
when she reads rubbish, she reads seriously,
throwing herself into what she reads, whereas a
man does not. Watch respectfully, because also
seriously, how a woman will regard a shelf of new
library novels from which she means to choose
one. She makes her choice quickly, as the man
of Scripture was bidden to sit down and write
quickly, and most likely she chooses well.

Mudie's business takes the form of thousands
of books circulating hither and thither, and never,
happily, all coming home at once, because there
would not be room to store them. They travel
overseas in tin-lined boxes so well made that on
occasion these have gone down into great waters

and been fished up again without harm befalling the contents.

There are also the "catacombs" below New Oxford Street in which Mudie stores his retired and retiring literary battalions. It is a sad and ghostly land of forgotten names and forgotten tomes, but, oh, so peaceful ! Nobody is there at night when the rats, inevitable under ground, sally forth, seeking literature to devour. Once their supper consisted of four novels entitled 'The Brilliant Peggy,' 'The Loves of Miss Anne,' 'Juicy Joe,' and 'Love Among the Ruins.' Why not ?

There were circulating libraries before Mudie's, but they were different—"moribund reservoirs," somebody described them, "of dry and old-fashioned novels." You will find them, and the using of them, satirized in Sheridan's play, 'The Rivals.' They were contracted little affairs, working meanly and inwardly, rather than outwardly, in the spacious spirit which should go with books. Here came the high idea of Charles Edward Mudie, begotten partly, perhaps, of the smallness of his father's newspaper shop down beside Cheyne Walk, in Chelsea, where Thomas Carlyle lived later, partly perhaps from reading Milton, or some other seer, on the right mission

of books. His idea was to scatter books, the
best books, the product of the nation's best brains,
by the thousand, nay, by the hundred thousand,
throughout London and the towns and villages
of the United Kingdom. He lived to do it and
it goes on, though he has been in his grave for
long.

Imagination is the parent of most large ventures
which succeed, because imagination means sim-
plicity. Mudie was a simple man, possessed by
a simple idea, and, once he had launched it, it
carried him far in the ocean of books and through
some strange adventures. He was not a man
who professed literature, but he was a good
reader, with a taste for poetry, and he had an
instinct for all books.

It was this, perhaps, as much as a sound grip
on the safe business road, which led him to be
named "Dictator of the London Literary World."
"So," Carlyle said to him at one of Lady Ash-
burnham's receptions, "you are the man who
undertakes to supply the world with books, to
divide the sheep from the goats ; a very serious
thing, eh ? "

Leave it to Mudie ! That came to be a saying, and he did his best to live up to it, always
bearing in mind that his responsibility was a busi-

ness in the form of a family library. Let a wolf in sheep's clothing creep into one of his boxes, let it go to some vicarage or quiet rural home, and where would he be ?

Mudie's was really by way of being a family newspaper which had a large circulation in the print and paper of other people. Naturally, in that circumstance, he elected for the safe line, even when some one might charge him with being unheroic. He was a librarian, not a hero ; but when he got books after his heart and his judgment, he could be all the hero, bold, venturesome, daring to a degree which made the old book-world of London hum with excitement.

"Why," sarcastically demanded an author who had felt Mudie's "tyranny," "didn't you refuse to circulate ' Bleak House ' because of the character of Mr. Chadband ? " The works of Dickens sold more widely than those of any other Victorian novelist, but much of their circulation was in " part form " and Mudie did not need so many as, in different circumstances, he would have done.

"Of course," he was upbraided, "you took thousands of ' Adam Bede ' on account of Dinah Morris, the beautiful Methodist ! " Poor man, he was apt to find himself wrong with some literary personage whatever he did, but that fear neither quenched his ardour nor his endurance, as the archives of his house, if you be admitted to their intimacy, make manifest.

When the third and fourth volumes of Macaulay's ' History of England ' appeared in December, 1855, he ordered two thousand five hundred copies of them. Fancy the stir this order made in the town department of our oldest publishers, the Longmans, of Paternoster Row. " Do you know the weight of this number ? You don't ! Well, the two volumes scale about seven pounds, so, if you add a few to the two thousand five hundred copies, you have a dead weight of nine tons. We can't deliver that in a hand-cart. Mudie will have to come and fetch his tons " ; and Mudie did.

Suppose, glancing over his archives, we record, in a simple but eloquent table, some of his other " big deals," thus :

1857, ' Livingstone's Travels in South Africa,' 3,500 copies.

1859, ' Tennyson's Idylls of the King,' 1,000 copies.

1861, ' Essays and Reviews ' (an anonymous work which made as much stir in its day as ' Lux Mundi ' did in ours), 2,000 copies.

1861, George Eliot's 'Silas Marner,' 3,000 copies.

1868, Queen Victoria's 'Journal of Our Life in the Highlands,' 1,000 copies.

1869, McClintock's 'Voyage of the *Fox*' in search of Franklin, 3,000 copies.

1878, Lady Brassey's 'Voyage of the *Sunbeam*,' 1,000 copies.

1880, Lord Beaconsfield's novel, 'Endymion, in three volumes, 3,000 copies.

Those deals were repeated in spirit during the 'nineties, though Charles Edward Mudie, the pioneer, could not longer make them ; for we find the library taking three thousand copies of Stanley's 'Darkest Africa,' a two-volume work, and two thousand five hundred copies of Lord Roberts's 'Forty-One Years In India,' also a two-volume book, at a large price. Of the 'Life of Tennyson,' by his son, Mudie's took two thousand and it made two volumes.

Nansen's 'Farthest North' begat an order for twelve hundred, Lord Morley's 'Gladstone,' in three volumes, one for a thousand, and Mr. Winston Churchill's biography of his father an order for a like number. Bear in mind always, that those were "advance orders," and therefore something of a gamble in what a particular book might

achieve with the public. You need to be a pro-
phet if you are to be a librarian, assuredly if you
are to be Mudie's.

Its record first call for a contemporary novel
was, probably, three thousand five hundred copies
of Sir Hall Caine's ' Christian,' now a dim spectre
on a fading horizon. With it there, and in figures
at Mudie's, is to be bracketed Miss Marie
Corelli's ' Master Christian,' of which three thousand copies were needed. But later, and higher,
comes Mrs. Humphry Ward's romance, ' The
Marriage of William Ashe ' with a Mudie record
of three thousand two hundred and sixteen copies.
Be it noted that Mrs. Ward was always a " best
circulator "—may this counterpart of " best
seller " be invented ?—at Mudie's, whose sound,
solid English tastes, interesting but " safe," she
well represented.

It was all different in the era of the comfortable
three-volume novel, which Mudie helped to
end, just because it had exhausted its mission.
While once it was, or was thought to be, a pillar
of the circulating library, it came to be a costly
burden. So in 1894 something happened, and
it died as a result of a " scrap of paper," signed,
first by Mr. Arthur O. Mudie, the chief of the
house, in succession to his father ; and then

by the other circulating libraries of London. There had been ' The Green Carnation,' for whose authorship a well-remembered name had been mentioned. On top of it came ' The Yellow Aster,' of Mrs. Mannington Caffyn, and it " boomed " in the most magnificent way. Mudie's kicked, on business grounds, about being left with enormous cargoes of " three-deckers," and out of that rumpus was born the six-shilling novel, which the war sent up to a higher figure. But the same brave, old flag, a true ensign to English reading, still flies over Mudie's—though you will see it on red letter days only !

XX

ALL THE KING'S ENGLISH

THEY will show you, at the Old Ashmolean, in Oxford, a postcard which catches the adventure, even the soul, of a great Oxford work. This has been the house and home of the ' Oxford English Dictionary,' a spacious book of the spacious language Shakespeare spake, nay, the supreme and enduring treasury of that language, now, itself, the chief vehicle of mental and material traffic among mankind.

The vagrant Old Ashmolean postcard found Sir James Murray, first editor, and, therefore, chief hero of the Dictionary, at Oxford years ago. Somebody made it by happening upon and then copying a passage from Jean Paul Richter's ' Levana.' " The writer of a dictionary," goes the postal extract, " rises every morning like the sun to move past some little star in his zodiac ; a new letter is to him a new year's festival, the conclusion of the old one, a harvest home."

Said Dr. John Brown of ' Rab and His Friends,'
" They are strange beings, these lexicographers " ; but he meant it lovingly, because,
like Richter, he would have known the spirit of
adventure which lies behind their labour, inspir-
ing it. The Oxford lexicographers have been
very willing to share the fun of this spirit, by
which is meant that " they are brothers, they are
men," communicative and humorous, as well as
learned.

They will, as a sort of *hors d'œuvre* to larger,
solider eating, dig you out a good joke against the
Old Ashmolean, and, therefore, against themselves, which one Macky plays in a volume of
' Journeys Through England,' dated 1722. He
was a Government agent, in plain language, a spy,
no doubt, and he is credited with first knowledge
of the second James's intention to come back.
What concerns us, however, and the Oxford
lexicographers is this Macky's visit to their abode
and his note, " The Museum Ashmoleanum
is adorned with a noble collection of natural
curiosities ! "

There was another traveller of about the same
time, who, resolving to see everything " curious
and worthy of observation " in Oxford, " went to
the museum vulgarly called the Nick Nackery."

Elias Ashmole's goods and chattels have been in a newer place, the present Ashmolean Museum, for years, and it is rather hard that those jeers should remain behind for the makers of the Dictionary.

Their long discipline in language has, however, given them a philosophy above even bad jokes, but they do remember a lawyer man who put his foot in it about the Old Ashmolean. He was pleading, for the University, that its assessment should be less than the tax-man wanted, and one of his arguments was, " You will understand that only slight, and not very valuable use is being made of the hall."

That was devil's advocacy, if you like, for the lexicographers, but they merely recall it with quiet scorn, and then repeat to you a delightful Dictionary story which Oxford invented and which Jowett may have liked, because it crawls into his ' Life and Letters.' Boswell meets Johnson in the Shades and asks him, " What would you say, sir, if you were informed that your dictionary is being superseded by the work of a Scotchman and a Nonconformist ? " " Sir," replies Johnson, " in order to be amusing it is not necessary to be flippant, inaccurate or indecent."

That brings us actively to Sir James Murray

and to the origins of the ' Oxford English Dictionary,' weary years ago. It had small beginnings,
though its staff became the " largest single engine
of research working anywhere," and those beginnings arose out of a gradual stress for knowledge.

Up to 1600 all the glossaries and dictionaries
in England were made to enable English folk to
learn another language, say, French, or Italian,
or Spanish. It had not occurred to anybody,
until the early years of the seventeenth century,
that an Englishman might want a dictionary the
better to understand his own language. But he
did need light on " ink-born terms " and " hard
words," and the realization of this brought along
Cawdrey and Cockeram and Bullohar, with their
little English dictionaries, first offerings in a high
sacrifice which has gone on ever since.

It was a red-letter day for English lexicography
when Samuel Johnson came into it, large worded,
sure of his power to club and cleave the language.
As Dr. Cragie, one of the " Dictionary " editors,
would tell you, among many other interesting
things, the great Sam introduced a new feature
into the English dictionary. He illustrated the
use of words by means of quotations from standard
authors, though he did not go back farther than
Spenser and Shakespeare.

When another good lexicographer, Richardson, arrived, he enlarged this method by going for quotations, in a liberal fashion, to the English writers of the Middle Ages. He also arranged his quotations in the order of their dates, which let students learn just how a word had changed with changing times. Now this, on a vaster scale, was to be the plan of the ' Oxford Dictionary,' as mapped out by its father, Dr. Murray.

It was in 1857 that Dean Trench, of Westminster, a scholar always associated with the " Queen's English," brought the Philological Society to attention by remarking on the inadequacy of the then existing dictionaries. Thousands of English words, he pointed out, had become obsolete, yet remained in the literature. But they had either quite escaped lexicographers or they had been excluded by the limitations of their various dictionaries. Especially there was no work that accounted for the history and meanings of words, from their origins onward through their developments.

The Philological Society took up the mission, and an army of scholarly volunteers set about examining the whole body of English literature. Duly a dictionary was projected, first under the editorship of Mr. Herbert Coleridge, then under

that of the many-sided Dr. Furnivall. He soon
saw that no sufficient dictionary could be made
until the mass of our early literature was examined,
and to that end he established the Early English
Text Society.

It was thus, from the learned loins of those
two bodies, the Philological Society and the Early
English Text Society, that the roots of the ' Oxford Dictionary ' sprang. There was the christ-
ening of it, all right, ' A New English Dictionary
on Historical Principles,' which became shortened
to ' N.E.D.' Much material was gathered for it
by English scholars everywhere and stored away,
but a certain despondency grew when years passed
and no publisher could be found to take on the
venture, which, indeed, was not to be wondered
at. But the Bridge of Sighs was crossed when
the Clarendon Press, of Oxford, handsomely
agreed to publish the Dictionary, which onwardly
some called ' Murray's Dictionary,' after the
editor, and all, eventually, the ' Oxford Dictionary.'

All human undertakings grow with time and
labour, and it is fortunate that their real magni-
tude is rarely seen at the start, otherwise they
might be left alone. Dean Trench and Mr. Herbert Coleridge thought their dear dictionary

could begin when a hundred thousand quotations had been put in order. Dr. Furnivall and Dr. Murray, thanks to the labours of thirteen hundred readers, got together three and a half million quotations, from the works of five thousand authors.

Steadily, for more than forty years the harvest went on, and to-day the Dictionary contains about a million and three-quarter printed quotations, from over five thousand authors. Completely, it extends to fully 15,000 pages, and these preserve some four hundred thousand words, though it might be rash to declare this the total verbal wealth of the English language.

May be Dominie Sampson had a vision of the 'Oxford Dictionary' on some occasion when he said "Prodeegious!" Anyhow, he would have thought well of his countryman, Dr. Murray, sitting down to it, in a little tin sort of house at Mill Hill. The agreement with the Clarendon Press was signed on March 1, 1879, in 1882 the first batch of "copy" was sent to the printers, and in February, 1884, the opening part of the dictionary saw the light.

By and by Dr. Murray moved to Oxford, a handier arrangement, and in a workshop of good space and light, but of no other pretensions, called

183

the Scriptorium, passed laborious days, weeks, months and years until his death in July, 1915. He had hoped to live and see the Dictionary finished on his eightieth birthday in 1917, but, as it is, one half of the monumental work stands to his direct credit, a wonderful achievement.

What friends Dr. Murray made through his far-flung task, what friends his colleagues and successors Dr. Henry Bradley, Dr. Cragie, and Mr. C. T. Onions, also made, and that alone is a good reward. To his " Scriptorium " would drift a letter from Tennyson about the word " balm cricket " which he had used, and which made etymological difficulties. George Eliot wrote concerning the word " Adust," which you may find in her ' Romola ' in the sense of " dusty." She thought it was the " feeling of rhythm which always accompanies my prose writing," that caused her to use the rarer word. Dr. Murray asked her how she wished to be quoted in the Dictionary, and she said always as " George Eliot," not by her real name. Many, many are the humanities, distinguished or not distinguished, which have been behind the great book, and they give colour to its romantic story.

How could it be otherwise with voluntary scholars at work in its interest, for over half a century, wherever the King's English runs and also in many foreign countries. Take a handful of their " scrip," yellowed by time, but carefully preserved at the Old Ashmolean, and think if it be not almost sacred. It speaks of men and women who may be dead and gone, or labouring still for the honour of our tongue.

There was that learned Dutchman, Mynheer Caland, whose interest in the work probably kept him alive, and who, for a long time, did not even get a complimentary copy of it. There was unknown Mrs. Moor, of the neat, carefully dated writing, who contributed from 1864 to 1866, and then just stopped. You wonder what happened to her and you are left wondering, because silence never answers, certainly not for a woman.

Good " readers " by the thousand the ' Oxford Dictionary ' has commanded and Dr. Brushfield was one of them, though he would spell Walter Raleigh, as " Ralegh " or " Ralley," or something like that, so leading somebody to say, " But you've knocked out Walter Raleigh's ' i '." Bad " readers " have been known, meaning those who, for all their enthusiasm, were careless in their quotations and, may be, neither began nor ended them.

These were pilers-up of trouble for the editorial

staff at headquarters, whose motto from the beginning was to gather wheat even from tares, to
examine everything and miss nothing having the
least illumination.   Fitzgerald Hall, a scholarly,
well-to-do American who dwelt in England, was
not a " reader " like that, for he gave assistance
of true value.   But he did have the sometimes
awkward peculiarity of writing on a grocer's
bill, a butcher's receipt or any old scrap of
paper.

Nothing, in fact or fiction, literature or life,
could be more dramatic, more strange than the
story of another American to whom the ' Oxford
Dictionary' genuinely owes much.   Something
of the story has leaked out, so there can be no
harm now in saying that the madman, for there
lies the drama, bore the name W. C. Minor.

He was a gentleman, a scholar and wealthy,
and somehow, in an image which one remembers
from Hugh Conway's famous " shocker,"
' Called Back,' the " sweet bells of his intellect "
became "jangled and out of tune."   He had, in
particular, the delusion that he was being tracked
down by people who wanted to harm him.   Accordingly he got hold of a revolver, for so far,
although the mental trouble was working, he was
a free man ; and one day, in London, thinking a

stranger was following him, he turned round and shot the stranger.

This led to Broadmoor, where the scholar in Minor survived, though otherwise he might be what he was. He put his case to the authorities of the asylum, saying that he was a student of the English language, that he wanted to contribute to the ' Oxford Dictionary ' then under way, and would they let him have facilities to work ? As he explained, he had the command of plenty of money, and therefore could pay, or have bought for him, any book he wanted, however rare and expensive.

He was given a room for study, and to it, ordered from catalogues and second-hand book-sellers, came early English works which the staff of the Dictionary could really not have afforded to buy. Minor went on for long, sending in his valuable " readings," always in copper-clear small writing, which you can curiously examine at the Old Ashmolean. Eventually his " slips," thanks to age and perhaps his malady, became faulty, and he went back to America to die.

A strange, true tale is it not ? But this big Dictionary has been a half a century expedition into the unknown wells of truth. There could have been no such expedition in any other country, for there would not have been the voluntary, learned diggers. Neither would there have been the wells to dig in, because what other language has the sweep of history, and the sweep of the globe, which belong to English?

Reflect that the grand adventure has settled for good the just place of each word in the successive strata of words which compose our language. Reflect also that each of those strata is not a mere matter of language, but a living witness to something vital in the history of the English race, for instance, the Norman Conquest with its French bearings. Thus to two things: that the 'Oxford Dictionary' has and holds our language, and that with its warp and woof there is intimately twined our history as a people.

An account of the 'Oxford English Dictionary' in all its aspects, would, as one of its editors has remarked, be an account not of a book only, but of the English language itself. Think how its wealth of material enables an impartial, final estimate of our authors to be made. Something which belongs to a man's time may have been attributed to himself, his "originality" may have been only the utterance of opinions and phrases all about him.

Again, take any section or cross-section of this

book of books, and instantly it pictures the English tongue as it was at a given date. You discover when the language was losing or making in riches of expression, and of that there are three outstanding ages, the fourteenth century, which had not before been sufficiently made clear, the sixteenth century, which we may call the Elizabethan age, and the second half of the nineteenth century, otherwise the Victorian age.

The splendid enrichment of English in our day has come very largely from the rise in what have been called " local schools " of English literature, carried to print in the novel chiefly, but also in poetry and the prose of fact. Some of us could put a hand on lovely dialect words in Thomas Hardy's Wessex novels, the classic instance of an English region yielding stories which are also universal to human nature.

Even more easily some of us could pick beautiful, purring Scots words from the book writings of Sir James Barrie and the other " kail-yarders " of sentimental years ago. Then modern science, as, for example, electricity or the " 'phone " and mechanics, as in the motor and the aeroplane, have thrown up a regiment of fresh words. New English language has, indeed, been in the making, and Armageddon contributed its share in scarlet letters, a tribute by the immortal dead to the mortal living.

One notable outcrop of the review of the English language by the ' Oxford Dictionary ' is the conferring of another glory on Sir Walter Scott. He had a wonderful memory, and the gift of using obsolete words which he came upon, with correctness of application. So, in his novels, he revived many English and some Scots words that had fallen into disuse. That is a distant but conclusive testimony to the generality and closeness with which the Waverley Novels were read as they appeared.

Moreover, even when the recovery of a word has not been definitely traced to Scott, he has earned the verdict that he probably had more to do with it than any other writer. " Henchman " he rescued from Captain Butt's ' Letters,' " raid," from old Border ballads or traditions, and if you know ' The Abbot ' intimately you will know that " a stricken field," which he employs there, was happened upon in a ballad and it meant simply " to strike a battle," or " a pitched battle."

Knowledge is impartial in judgment and, for all its appreciation of Scott, the ' Oxford Dictionary ' has had a crow to pluck with him, one at least. There is a watchmaker character, David

Ramsay, in the 'Fortunes of Nigel' and Scott makes him work out some calculations, the wording of which came for analysis to a " Dictionary " man. He looked up " retort " in the third edition, completed in 1797, of the ' Encyclopædia Britannica ' and he found that Scott had done the same ; but, alas, he had copied his technical inspiration all wrong.

Similarly, Dean Swift went for a nautical description which occurs in ' Gulliver,' to Sturmy's ' Mariner's Magazine ' of 1669, and his cloth made his plagiarism rank, as well as rampant. There is no escaping the ' Oxford Dictionary,' which has even proved that the kind of overcoat known as a " Spencer " was so named, not after the third Earl Spencer, as is commonly given, but after the second Earl, who was born in 1758.

The ' O.E.D.' is not an institution to which, as old Richardson said of early dictionaries, " idleness may fly for instantaneous relief from ignorance." It is far too great in its river of contents for that, but a right scholar, knowing how to pierce behind the veil, might make a good book of anecdotage from its revelations. Who first used the word " velocimeter," meaning a device for measuring velocities ? It was Herbert Spen-

191

cer, in an article he wrote when he was more engineer than philosopher.

How do we now happen to speak of " spindrift," instead of the older " spoondrift " when we signify fine spray driven before the wind ? Well, " spindrift " was used in south-west Scotland simply because there they say " spin " for " spoon," and William Black, a Glasgow man, put it into his stories, from which, apparently, it has passed into the common usage we make of it to-day. Nothing is wonderful when you know, and the ' O.E.D.' knows ever such a lot.

It knows how to spell and elucidate " incircumscriptibleness," and " honorificabilitudinity," and " antidisestablishmentarians," champion long English words, the last from the mouth of Archbishop Benson. It knows that a lexicographer makes light work of " parallelepiped " and " supralapsarian " and that his powers of discovery and discrimination are seriously taxed when he comes to words like " wealth " and " work," " war " and " waste," " wild " and " wilful." You would have supposed it the contrary, would you not ?

But the lexicographer has his hard days with the common words, the vital words, those that have been on the tongues of the race since they began to speak the language. Thus " Get " fills twenty-two columns of the ' Dictionary ' and is divided into seventy-three senses, with numerous subdivisions. " Give " needs twenty-five columns, and " Gro " thirty-five, but " Set " calls for fifty-five columns and develops a hundred and fifty numbered sections, not to speak of subsections.

Some day, perhaps, the ' Oxford Dictionary,' like the Oxford Bible, will be making a standing offer of a guinea to anybody who can discover an error in it. People do write making such discoveries but mostly they turn out mare's nests, or worse, if worse be possible. The wrong thing has been looked at, or it has been read wrongly ; but now and then, of course, a point of real correction does come along, and, after confirmation, it is gratefully accepted.

Naturally a work in which taking pains has been carried to the height of genius, is already accepted, in legislature and law court, in study and library, as the authoritative oracle on the English language. What it says goes, an American expression that also applies to the position of the ' Dictionary ' across the waters of the Atlantic, which it helps mightily to bridge. The making of this bridge in the good time of forty odd years has cost the Oxford Press a quarter of a million sterling. But that news, if you please, may only be whispered as between two Anglo-Saxon peoples equally proud of the glory which is the English language.

POSTSCRIPT

This book has been built out of writings contributed from time to time, as the occasion inspired, to " The Graphic," " The Strand Magazine," " The Daily Graphic " and especially to " The Girl's Own Paper and Woman's Magazine," and the courtesy of their present use is warmly acknowledged by the author.